# The Single Ladies' Commandments
## Songs for Love, Healing, Freedom, and Purpose

**90 DAILY DEVOTIONS**

## By: Jasmine Jones

*The Commandments Series*

The Single Ladies' Commandments
Songs for Love, Healing, Freedom, and Purpose
Published by J Squared Productions

Cover design by Sydney Pea
Cover photo by Darren Clark

ISBN: 978-0-6928401-9-1
ISBN: 978-1-7328290-0-8 (ebook)

1. Single Women–Religious Life. 2. Christian Ladies–Religious Life. 3. Self-Help–Spiritual Life. 4. Religious aspects–Christianity. 5. Husbands–Christian Life.
Printed in the United States of America.
2016
10 9 8 7 6 5 4 3 2

For information, questions, scheduling, or details about upcoming books in The Commandments Series, please contact the author at the email provided: info@jasminejones.co, or visit www.jasminejones.co.

**Dedication**
To my future husband:
I have faith that being obedient to this process–God's process,
brings me closer to complete healing and closer to you.

# Table of Contents

# Introduction

Why **90** songs? Why a **90**-day guide for better love, healing, freedom, and purpose? The answer lies in this, *Single Ladies*, **90** days commits you to a level of responsibility. It requires you to take ownership of your own love life, rectify your own healing, and make the conscious choice to live free and on purpose. Imagine being free from every past thing and every past experience that has bound you. Imagine having the power and wisdom to embrace your learned lessons. What better way to make your imagination a reality than through music?

These daily devotions are designed to inspire you to embrace and manage your life experiences through the artistic medium of music. Think about it. At some point or another, music have roused just about every emotion from inside of you–laughter, tears, anger, joy, and pain. Music urges you to dance and sing, and it serves as a personal reflection of your everyday life. From this devotional book, you will learn to engage a great familiarity to you, that familiarity is your interest and love for music. You will then use your knowledge to embrace the love of God in your life and enhance your spiritual journey.

This guide illustrates daily applicative examples to help you achieve and fulfill *The Singles Ladies' Commandments*, the first installment in the Commandments Series. Memorize your *Singles Ladies' Commandments* and apply them to your daily walk, experiences,

1

and encounters. As you read each of your 90 devotions, reference the following commandments:

**Commandment #1:** Thou shall *love* God and thyself.

**Commandment #2:** Thou shall accept and receive inward spiritual *healing*.

**Commandment #3:** Thou shall live in unadulterated *freedom, freedom* from every past thing and situation.

**Commandment #4:** Thou shall find *purpose* and live on *purpose*.

Each daily devotion is comprised of three main sections: **Listen**, **Read**, and **Reference**.

For each daily devotion, you are encouraged to seek a reliable, lawful, and permissible music listening application and listen to a radio edited or clean version of the listed song. If you have access to Spotify or Apple Music, you may choose to subscribe to www.jasminejones.co for a website link to *The Single Ladies' Commandments* playlist, which includes a collection of songs in this book. Keep in mind additional subscription rates to the music listening application may apply.

Following the music, you will read the daily devotion for understanding and reference the biblical scripture. You are encouraged to reference the source of all the biblical scriptures for further personal study.

*Single Ladies*, be prepared for the next **90** days of responsibility as God teaches you how to wisely use the days He has given you.

So teach *us* to number our days,

That we may gain a heart of wisdom.

– Psalm **90**:12 (NKJV)

# Commandment #1

# *Love*

Thou shall love God and thyself.

## Day 1: Looking For Love

**Listen**

Mary J. Blige – Real Love (1992)

**Read**

Stop searching right now at this very instant; you don't need to search for love. Two reasons: God is real love and searching for love is a man's job. God is the definition of love. That means you don't need to go roaming or searching the Earth for real love. When you are ready to seek God, God's love and presence is at your disposal. When you seek God, you will find Him, and when you find God, you will find real love.

Now, let's have a heart to heart about the second reason. Do you know those status updates you post on social media? The ones that ask you, "what's on your mind?" or "how are you feeling?" Yes, these. Please *Single Ladies*, I beg of you, do not ever respond with *looking for love*. God did not intend for you to search for love, not high or low, not above or beneath. There are plenty of meticulous tasks that we can do that men are not expected to do–like enduring nine months of pregnancy, experiencing childbirth, or blaming it on PMS, but looking for love is not one of them.

Honestly, I am quite relieved. Can you imagine the pressure men must bear? A wife is a gift to man from God; a tangible sign that he received favor from the Lord. Hence, why would you attempt to deprive a man from receiving his favor? Is it because you're a modern-day woman? Truth is that is not an admirable quality of a modern-day woman. That is the quality of a woman attempting to take love into her own hands when her first responsibility is to seek God's real love.

**Reference**

*He who* finds a wife finds a good *thing,*

And obtains favor from the Lord.

– Proverbs 18:22 (NKJV)

## Day 2: Who's Going To Love These Flaws?

**Listen**

Beyoncé – Flaws and All (2007)

**Read**

Have you ever lain awake alone at night dreaming of the perfect man to love you with all your flaws? I can't be alone on this one, *Single Ladies*. You lie awake with one eye open, wishing and praying for that one man who can piece together all your imperfect pieces perfectly. You long for a man who will daily accept your excessive talking, inherent nagging, and even your not so occasional attitude. Not to mention, a man who will see past every physical imperfection that you can't help but stare into the mirror to critique–small boobs, flat butt, blemished skin, and crooked smile.

We dare to dream that one day a man will slay the dragon just for the sole purpose and privilege of loving and accepting us with all our flaws, right? Maybe a little over zealous, but you get the point. When we lay awake at night, we often fail to realize one fact, it typically doesn't cross our minds that someone already loves and accepts us even far more than we can imagine. God chose you with all your faults, even before you were conceived in your mother's womb. God loves you now, even in this very moment. He accepts you and He desires for you to reciprocate His love through seeking and honoring Him. Next time you lay awake at night, yearning for a faultless love, smile, and thank the Lord. Tell God you are grateful for His faultless love!

## Reference

Even before he made the world, God loved us and chose us in Christ to be holy and without fault in His eyes.

– Ephesians 1:4 (NLT)

## Day 3: Pay the Toll

**Listen**

Beyoncé – Single Ladies (Put A Ring On It) (2008)

**Read**

We may not understand why he didn't love us or maybe even why he didn't like us. We may not understand why he ended the relationship or why he cheated. However, we do know that we must swallow one large, painful pill. There's no gaining x-ray vision to see straight through that elephant in the room. That elephant's name is *You.* That's right, *You!* You sing the song and wave that left hand in the air with style and pride. Once the song is over, you realize deep down that you have no choice but to admit that he didn't want you. You can make all the excuses you want for him–he was young, immature, or wasn't ready to settle down. When truth is, a man who *liked it*– who liked you, would commit a lifetime with you, never allowing anything to stand in his way.

　　Do you know, *Single Ladies,* that God loved you so much that He paid the highest toll because your worth is far greater than any precious jewel? You can find solace in this fact. You are more precious than any stone in any ring that any man can place on your ring finger. Just envision *the one* you thought was the one, on a highway where all signs lead to you, but first he was required to pay the toll to gain access to you. The reason that man could not gain full access to your highway may very well be that he couldn't afford your toll. Understanding only God knows the real reason, just be patient for the man who is more than willing to pay your toll. Believe me, *Single Ladies*, I understand, it's easier said than done.

**Reference**

Who can find a virtuous and capable wife?

She is more precious than rubies.

Her husband can trust her,

and she will greatly enrich his life.

– Proverbs 31:10-11 (NLT)

## Day 4: Scared of Love?

**Listen**

Jazmine Sullivan – Lions, Tigers & Bears (2008)

**Read**

Over and over again, you may feel like you lost in the game of love. You may feel as if you are incapable of opening up to another man. You can't even phantom another attempt to gain love. Just processing the thought of starting over floods you with emotions. An emotional overflow of fear and terror fills your mind. The fear of love then far outweighs the thought and possibility of receiving genuine love because your heart feels broken into pieces. You feel incapable of loving again, but this is only because your view of love has been tainted.

Think of love like currency. The enemy, also known as Satan who rebelled against God (Ezekiel 28:14-18), has attempted to exchange your view of love with fear. These two currencies are not interchangeable; in fact, there's no existing exchange rate between these two currencies. Take fear to the bank right now and try to exchange it for love. The bank teller may laugh in your face. You have been trained to associate love with fear, but these entities belong to two separate and non-interchangeable origins. God is *love, power, and a sound mind*, while fear is not of God (2 Timothy 1:7). Remember, you are promised all that *is* of God. Find yourself wrapped up in the things of God and fear will have no space to flourish in your bank account.

**Reference**

For God has not given us a spirit of fear, but of power and of love and of a sound mind.

– 2 Timothy 1:7 (NKJV)

## Day 5: Cardiac Arrest

**Listen**

Trey Songz – Heart Attack (2012)

**Read**

What do you do when you feel you can't talk to anyone and your heart is heavy and burdensome? When the man you love doesn't want to hear it, and the people who love you can't know the truth for fear they might judge you. How do you keep it all inside when you're waiting to burst and let it all out or when you're sick of hiding and want to come out? What happens when you're ready to seek, but the one you love doesn't want to be found?

*Single Ladies*, what do you do when you can't survive without him? When you're flat lining because he doesn't reciprocate your love? God will be your defibrillator and shock your heart back into rhythm. At that moment, you'll recognize that God's heart beats for you. You'll recognize that love isn't supposed to resemble a heart attack. God is concerned about you and He will never leave you. You will desire to reciprocate His love and you will seek it daily. When you knock on the Kingdom's doors in prayer, the doors will open. On the other side, you will find God's heart and His unyielding love waiting for you.

**Reference**

Keep on asking, and you will receive what you ask for. Keep on seeking, and you will find. Keep on knocking, and the door will be opened to you.

– Matthew 7:7 (NLT)

# Day 6: Let Me See You Do That Dance

**Listen**

Maroon 5 – She Will Be Loved (2002)

**Read**

John 3:16 is one of the most popular verses of Christian biblical scriptures. As Christians, we sometimes take this scripture for granted. I am not alluding that we take God's love or Jesus' sacrifice for granted. We understand Jesus died an agonizing death, so we have the chance of eternal life. We appreciate God's undying love for us, so we repay Him with our own life through striving to live daily in His image.

If you ever learned a dance routine, you'll appreciate this analogy. When a dancer learns choreography, she learns in steps. She learns the cues in the music. She listens for beats, tempos, and lyrics. She practices the first steps using the cues as her aid. Once she learns the first few steps, she repeats this technique for the next set of steps, and then the next until the routine becomes second nature. Once she's comfortable with the routine, she may not even practice anymore. However, what happens when she doesn't practice? She loses it, right? Consequently, she starts practicing again and her instincts kick in. She is able to recall her previously learned steps; only this time, she incorporates finishing touches, perfecting the routine.

In most of our beginning stages of our Christian walk, we learned John 3:16. Now, we could see this scripture and simply glance over it. We know this scripture, right? The beauty in God's word is that it is living; you can apply it to your everyday life including your thoughts and desires (Hebrews 4:12). The word of God is like the dance routine; it's learned once, but when it's relearned, you are able to perfect it and make it your own. You can even apply it to your desire for a man of God, a man who will love you unconditionally. A man who wants to love you; in fact, he embraces loving you.

The word of God is about application. Every day you should apply the word to your life. You're waiting for a man of God, but how should this man love you? He should love you as God loves you. He should love you as Jesus loves you. If necessary, he is willing to wait in the pouring rain for you. Like God, he should not leave your side in times of trouble (Deuteronomy 31:8). In times of danger, he is willing to lay down his life for you. This is true chivalry; any man can open doors, pull out a chair, or pay for a date. These qualities are appreciated, but a man who demonstrates true chivalry is a man of valor. The next time you come across a popular verse of a scripture, instead of dismissing it as second nature, remind yourself of God's living word, and find the application to your present day.

**Reference**

For God so loved the world that He gave His only begotten Son, that whoever believes in Him should not perish but have everlasting life.

– John 3:16 (NKJV)

## Day 7: Imprisoned

**Listen**

Brandy – Almost Doesn't Count (1998)

**Read**

He almost chose me. He almost loved me. Brandy's titled song said it best, *almost doesn't count*. When I was nine years old, this was my favorite song. Lord knows I didn't understand the true message, nor could I relate to the concept of halfway loving someone. I enjoyed singing the chorus and loved the melody. I would sing along using the lyrics in the CD's booklet. In 1998, dialing up the Internet to access the song lyrics was not a convenience in my household. I memorized all the lyrics since the song was on repeat all-day long.

This is a perfect example of taking something as second nature for granted. More recently, I recognized another message in this song. A message that relates to Paul; he was standing on trial appearing before King Agrippa as presiding judge (Acts 26:1). For a chance of freedom, Paul provided his testimony, his God-given testimony. He shared his experience as a persecutor of Christians until the day God opened his eyes, and he began evangelizing to many people (Acts 26:12-18). Following Paul's testimony, King Agrippa issued the verdict, "You almost persuaded me to become a Christian" (Acts 26:28 NKJV).

Like Brandy explained almost wasn't enough, Paul was

19

shipped to prison (Acts 27:1). If King Agrippa were convinced to become a Christian, he would understand that God called us as one in His body (Ephesians 4:4). He would have been humbling, patient, loving, and most of all, forgiving (Ephesians 4:2). He would have understood that many people in the world attempt to spiritually imprison those serving God and there was no need to physically imprison Paul.

Jesus told us one can't serve two masters, one will be hated and the other loved (Matthew 6:24). King Agrippa would have considered dropping Paul's charges if he had not disagreed with Caesar (Acts 26:32). King Agrippa could not worship God, and the nation, so he chose the nation. Don't be like King Agrippa; almost choosing or loving God is not enough. You must choose Him above all things!

**Reference**

[There is] one Lord, one faith, one baptism,
 one God and Father of all,
who is over all, in all, and living through all.
– Ephesians 4:5-6 (NKJV)

## Day 8: The Reciprocal

**Listen**

Disclosure feat. Sam Smith – Latch (2013)

**Read**

There was a woman who escaped an abusive relationship. She found herself living all alone in the wooded hills. Every day she walked 5 miles into town for her basic essentials and 5 miles back home. A man noticed her and fell in love with her at first sight. He desired to demonstrate his love for the woman. One day, while she was in town, he drove to her home in the hills and left her a bicycle. She returned home and spotted the bicycle. The next day, she walked the bicycle into town. The man noticed her right away. He asked if she liked her new bicycle, and revealed he was the donor. The woman angrily returned the bicycle to the man, and then turned around to walk back home.

She was upset that the man would give her such a gift without even asking her. The woman had been controlled in her previous abusive relationship so long, that she viewed the man's gesture as an act of control. On her walk, she realized she was very rude to the man, when perhaps this man was genuine. The next day, she walked into town and she had a heart to heart with the man. She apologized for her actions, and began to walk away.

"Aren't you forgetting something?" the man asked, pointing

to the bicycle.

"Yes," she smiled in response.

She seated herself on the bicycle and rode her bicycle back home. From that day forward, the man and woman grew closer and closer, and inevitably, she fell in love with him too.

Should you ask to latch onto a man's love? A man, who desires to love you, will show you love, no need to ask for it. Like the man in the story, God has already shown you His love. Understand love is a reciprocal. If you desire a closer relationship with Him, you must reciprocate His love for you. You show love, and then you gain love. When you pray, read your bible, and offer praises to God, you find yourself closer to God.

In mathematics, what makes a reciprocal, a reciprocal? A reciprocal is just a number upside down. When that number is a reciprocal of another number the product is one. For instance: $\frac{1}{2}$ multiplied by 2 equals 1. If you're meeting God halfway, He will meet you with the reciprocal creating a value of one! You will find yourself locked in God's love, *one* with the Father!

**Reference**

Come close to God, and God will come close to you . . .

– James 4:8 (NLT)

## Day 9: Take The Plunge

**Listen**

Jazmine Sullivan – Forever Don't Last (2015)

**Read**

Forever doesn't last *forever.* We live in a world where marriage is declining, cohabitation is inclining, and divorce rates are moving steadily upward. You may notice your unmarried friends in relationships today, but out of relationships tomorrow. We jump in and quickly jump out of relationships and marriages. *This is nothing new under the sun* (Ecclesiastes 1:9 NKJV). In ancient times, people conducted themselves in the same manner (Ecclesiastes 1:10). Yet, even in ancient times, people still plunged into the deep end of marriage knowing these facts.

Are they crazy? Why even marry? *Single Ladies,* you have God on your side. You don't participate in the world's methods. Therefore, any God ordained marriage, involving you and your husband, is sanctified and holy. Don't fear marriage having witnessed your parents' marriage crumble right before your eyes. Perhaps your parents never married and life worked out just fine for them. They either cohabitated, or just moved on and lived separate, happy lives.

Be honest with yourself, would you deny your own blessing? God created a man who loves Jesus Christ first, and will love you unconditionally. Would you deny this man? Marriage is a blessing from God. Will you tell God, *no, I don't want this blessing?* In the past, I denied my own blessing. I allowed fear to consume my thoughts but now God's wisdom abides in my thoughts.

Understanding forever doesn't last *forever.* Do you know that even God ordained marriages have an expiration date? All marriages will surely end, but a God ordained marriage, will not end in divorce. Instead, it will end when one spouse departs to Heaven. If marriage ends when one spouse departs to Heaven, why marry?

The sun has existed almost as long as the Earth; it has borne witness to many things. One of which is the burden of this life. We have marriage on this Earth to ease the burdens of life, and endure life under the sun (Ecclesiastes 9:9). In Heaven, these burdens do not exist; therefore, a husband is not essential in Heaven.

You may question, will I not see my husband in Heaven? You may certainly pass him on the streets of gold, but he will no longer be your husband. In Heaven, you will be like the angels who don't marry (Matthew 22:30). There is *one* thing that will last forever in Heaven, that's you!

Jesus told us, "For whoever desires to save his life will lose it, but whoever loses his life for My sake will find it" (Matthew 16:25 NKJV).

Anything on this Earth will surely fade away, only those who find themselves in the will of God will find forever (1 John 2:17). Marriage and this world will fade away, but have confidence that life with *Jesus Christ is the same yesterday, today, and forever* (Hebrews 13:8 NKJV).

## Reference

Surely goodness and mercy shall follow me

All the days of my life;

And I will dwell in the house of the Lord

Forever.

– Psalm 23:6 (NKJV)

## Day 10: The Real Me

**Listen**

Bruno Mars – Just The Way You Are (2010)

**Read**

You meet a guy maybe in passing, maybe at school or at work, or maybe even through a mutual friend. You start to date him, but you begin to wonder, *is this guy really into me? I mean, the real me.* Of course, he compliments you in every way imaginable; the way your hair falls, your big smile, and your sweet face, but you question, if that is all he sees? Does he only see you for your outer beauty? After all, men are visual and physically driven creatures so how do you obtain the answer?

Consider the biblical story of David. His father had sevens sons, the youngest being David, who merely tended sheep (1 Samuel 16:10-11). David was considered among the least of his brothers in terms of physical stature, but God chose and anointed David as king (1 Samuel 16:7). A king is often regarded as physically strong and powerful, so why did God choose David? Here's the answer: God looks at the heart and God had a clear scope into David's heart. God declared that David was a man after His own heart (Acts 13:22).

The husband created for you is also a man after God's own heart. That means he desires daily to live a life that is pleasing in the Lord's sight. That man is so in tune with God that he thinks like God. That man will see you, the real you! Not just your outer appearance, but also and most importantly, your inner beauty–your heart.

## Reference

" . . . For the Lord does not see as man sees; for man looks at the outward appearance, but the Lord looks at the heart."

– 1 Samuel 16:7 (NKJV)

## Day 11: Unpretty

**Listen**

J. Cole feat. TLC – Crooked Smile [Clean] (2013)

**Read**

*Pretty is as pretty does.* This means you're only as pretty, or beautiful as your actions. Your actions are a direct reflection of your heart. It's not your outside appearance, but rather what's inside of you, that defines you. This means that a crooked smile doesn't define you. This doesn't mean you can't use tools to correct it. Braces were created for that very reason. Whatever you have, thank God for it.

The same concept can be applied to how you view men. We talked about how God sees a man's heart versus his physical appearance. We should do the same. That doesn't mean you cast down your own desires or settle for a man. Just remember to look at the whole package. What are his inner makings? Does he *pursue righteousness, godliness, faith, love, patience, and gentleness* (1 Timothy 6:11 NKJV)? Choose a man with qualities that defines character.

Consider your inner makings as well. Growing up, I enjoyed watching horror films. Against my better judgment, I accompanied a date to watch a horror film full of murder and gloom. After the movie, I felt troubled and quite tense. I quickly discovered I no longer desired to watch those horror films I once enjoyed. I understood the toll the film was taking on my inner woman–my

28

spirit. As you draw closer to God, you may also find that the things you used to do, you no longer desire to do. This is not because you literally can't do it.

Your eyes can't easily receive those things because they do not line up with your inner self. Your eyes' gates are a direct connection to your spirit. When your eyes are exposed to things that are corrupt, you may also become corrupt or disturbed on the inside (Luke 11:34). If your eyes receive things that are righteous, you will exuberate righteousness (Luke 11:34).

In the same token, the things that you hear may affect you. Can you recall a time when a man emotionally wounded you and you played a heartbreak song? You play the song because you can relate to it. Be careful not to stay in that place. You may find that all you have is heartbreak.

Have you ever paid attention to the evolution of an artist's repertoire? Artists like Mary J. Blige and Beyoncé had record-breaking albums composing of some of the best breakup songs in the 90's and the 2000's. When these women matured and initially married, you may have noticed a different tone in their songs. Following the change in their life's events, you may have noticed the songs were filled with more messages of love, empowerment, life, and fun, but not as many breakup songs. Think about the reasoning behind this change. If you were newly married, would you want to sing about heartbreak and love loss? You probably would not.

Music can affect our moods. Music can reflect how we feel; it can also cause us to stay stuck in place—a place where we do not feel peace, but distress. One example of this is that of a distraught Saul. Whenever David played the harp, Saul would no longer feel troubled, he felt anew (1 Samuel 16:23). If you desire love, instead of listening to songs of heartbreak, listen to songs that engage you in happiness and love! Be the peaceful you that God called you to be.

**Reference**

"But you, O man of God, flee these things and pursue righteousness, godliness, faith, love, patience, gentleness"

– 1 Timothy 6:11 NKJV

## Day 12: Mickey vs. Goofy

**Listen**

Christina Aguilera – Fighter (2002)

**Read**

Mickey Mouse was my favorite animated character as a child. Mickey Mouse had personality and charisma. He had the character of a gentleman. He treated Minnie Mouse with such respect and affection. I always admired these *gentlemanly* qualities, even at a young age. Somehow, along the way, I lost sight of these admired qualities in men and ended up with Goofy after Goofy. Goofy is a man who has no regards for you as a woman. Goofy doesn't take you seriously and worst of all, he's clumsy with your heart.

Be honest with yourself. You don't like how Goofy is treating you, but you defend him. He's not like the other men from your past; he's different. You have chemistry, or a *deep* connection, when he's likely just a *paper man* bluffing as a quality man. What's a *paper man*? A man who has his whole life in order on paper, his résumé is quite flattering and impressive. You think you can employ him because he has the education, the career, and the nice house, but that's all he is; he's *paper*. He doesn't respect you and he's not the best quality man for you. Perhaps you're thinking every other woman is propositioned with an engagement ring and your biological clock is ticking, but don't be afraid that your Mickey won't come along. You don't need

31

Goofy. You can do better. Be a woman of substance. Be a woman who appreciates substance.

A woman of substance doesn't choose to hate Goofy. Instead, you forgive him as God forgives you daily (Matthew 6:14-15). Your heart may feel shattered, but he didn't destroy you. You are a fighter! Don't think of this moment as the worst experience. Think of it as a learning experience. He may not love you, but you're stronger because of it. You had to experience this metamorphosis; how else would you have evolved from a caterpillar to a butterfly? Metamorphosis was a necessary process for you to appreciate love just a little more so now you recognize the beauty of love. Find comfort that one day you'll have God-ordained love! Forgive him because in forgiveness comes your healing and it builds your wisdom.

I forgave Goofy because holding onto bitterness was only destroying me. Goofy was off living his carefree life. Don't be bitter, don't despise, don't anger, and don't speak evil (Ephesians 4:31). Remember, it's all about forgiveness.

**Reference**

Let all bitterness, wrath, anger, clamor, and evil speaking be put away from you, with all malice. And be kind to one another, tenderhearted, forgiving one another, even as God in Christ forgave you.
– Ephesians 4:31-32 (NKJV)

# Day 13: Welcome Home

**Listen**

Chrisette Michele – Love Won't Leave Me Out (2013)

**Read**

Imagine your heart as a home. When the door to your heart is wide open, you welcome love inside. When you close and lock the door of your heart, and then throw away the key, love can't enter. You're afraid to welcome another man inside. You throw away the key to ensure no other man has an opportunity to hurt you. When you harden your heart nothing can enter, even the positive things you desire in your life can't enter. When you close the door of your heart, the Spirit of God, blessings, forgiveness, and harvest can't enter and dwell in your home. You certainly can't accept genuine love from your future husband with a hardened heart. Since you lost the key to your hardened heart, only one locksmith is capable of opening your heart. That locksmith is Jesus. The only way to obtain His services is by accepting the love of God at your heart's door.

Now let's talk about what is beyond the door of your home. It is a beautiful concept to dream of everything you've ever imagined for your perfect home. You don't spend hours watching home and garden television in vain. You desire a white picket fence, a beautiful garden, a two-car garage, a stunning kitchen with a fully stocked refrigerator, and a welcome mat under a ruby red door. Of course, you dream of the things inside your home—a home filled with love, a husband, children, and a brown-spotted dog. Just the thought of this home creates a sense of joy and gratefulness. It's perfectly normal to have these desires, but possess this same sense of gratitude when you enter the house of the Lord (Psalm 100:4). God welcomes us into His presence with open arms. He desires we dwell in His home forever (Psalm 23:6). If you desire that earthly home, learn how to appreciate God's presence.

*Understand faith without works is dead* (James 2:14-18 NKJV). Demonstrate faith in believing you will receive the home with a white picket fence, a welcome mat, and a garden, through showing you appreciate being in God's home.

If you desire the husband and children, consider mirroring the faithfulness of Ruth. She was only one of two women to have her name grace a book of the Holy Bible. Ruth's husband passed away, yet she chose to return home with her mother-in-law, Naomi, instead of returning to her parents' home (Ruth 1:5, Ruth 1:16-17). Her faithfulness gave her favor with Boaz, a wealthy man, who showed kindness toward a meager Ruth (Ruth 2:1, Ruth 2:10-11). At least two seasons had passed, still Ruth did not lose faith God would bless her with another husband (Ruth 2:23). As her mother-in-law instructed, Ruth exhibited faith and laid at Boaz's feet all night showing loyalty to him (Ruth 3:4, Ruth 3:14). Boaz recognized her faithfulness. He married Ruth and from their union, she was blessed with a son (Ruth 4:13).

Perhaps you're a woman who already exhibits this level of faithfulness. Act on your faithfulness wisely. Not every man deserves your loyalty. As women, sometimes we are loyal to a fault. Recognize Goofy doesn't deserve your faithfulness. Notice Boaz was first genuinely kind to Ruth before she laid at his feet. First and foremost, be loyal to your principles. Don't deny your faithfulness to God and His teachings while being loyal to any man. A man who deserves your faithfulness respects your covenant with God first.

On the other hand, do not close your heart to faithfulness either. Ruth was not afraid to open up her heart again. Despite the fact her first husband died, she believed love would welcome her into its home again. If you desire to love without fear, meditate on this Psalm:

*The Lord is my light and my salvation;*
*Whom shall I fear?*
*The Lord is the strength of my life;*
*Of whom shall I be afraid?*
(Psalm 27:1 NKJV).

Allow God to unharden your heart to receive His love and all His blessings that come along with love (Ezekiel 36:26). Love has not forgotten about you. Before you know it, love will announce the words, *Welcome Home!*

**Reference**

Therefore, having been justified by faith, we have peace with God through our Lord Jesus Christ through whom also we have access by faith into this grace in which we stand, and rejoice in hope of the glory of God. And not only *that*, but we also glory in tribulations, knowing that tribulation produces perseverance; and perseverance, character; and character, hope. Now hope does not disappoint because the love of God has been poured out in our hearts by the Holy Spirit who was given to us.

– Romans 5:1-5 (NKJV)

## Day 14: Wait For Love

**Listen**

Trip Lee – Looking For Love (2006)

**Read**

As *Single Ladies*, we understand that we shouldn't be looking for love, but when love comes for you, how do you know what it looks like? We may have declared to a guy or two that we loved them, but once the smoke is clear and we come off our high, we start to question if it was love at all? Maybe it was just strong feelings or infatuation.

Recognize the definition of love in God. *Single Ladies, love is patient, kind, not boastful, or rude* (1 Corinthians 13:4-5 NLT). God is love and He exhibits all these characteristics. A man that comes for you in the name of love should exhibit love in his every encounter. He should love his neighbor and even love his enemies.

As Jesus declares, *you shall love your neighbor as yourself. There is no other commandment greater than these* (Mark 12:31 NKJV).

Jesus also instructed *love your enemies! Pray for those who persecute you* . . . (Matthew 5:44 NLT).

If that man is not exhibiting the characteristics of love to all, he may not be capable of loving you either. Wait for a love that's worth your energy; a love that that endures all. Wait for a love that doesn't give up at the first sight of trouble. Wait for a love that is sincere. Wait for love, *Single Ladies!*

37

**Reference**

Love is patient and kind. Love is not jealous or boastful or proud or rude. It does not demand its own way. It is not irritable, and it keeps no record of being wronged. It does not rejoice about injustice but rejoices whenever the truth wins out. Love never gives up, never loses faith, is always hopeful, and endures through every circumstance.

– 1 Corinthians 13:4-7 (NLT)

# Commandment #2

# *Healing*

Thou shall accept and receive
inward spiritual healing.

## Day 15: Healing Your Heels?

**Listen**

Drake feat. Swizz Beatz & T.I. – Fancy [Clean] (2010)

**Read**

We all know it hurts to walk in heels and all things heal in time, but do you ever stop to think about the reality of the healing process? Take this time to think about it. Have you ever experienced the discomfort of wearing an excruciating painful pair of heels? You may have purchased those fancy heels at the store a half size too small because it was the last size on the sale's rack. Perhaps the heels were only sold in a narrow fit, but your mother *blessed* you with wide feet. Yet, you still had to purchase those last pair of heels.

You find yourself walking in heels that don't fit quite right. *Single Ladies*, you shouldn't force those heels to fit, especially when you can acknowledge that those heels are the establishing source of your pain and your bunions. Being proactive to prevent self-inflicted pain is a choice. It takes a sense of self-awareness to be honest with yourself before you force those painful shoes on your feet. Ask yourself, is this inevitable, painful outcome worth a few fleeting moments of *beauty*? Is it worth being fancy?

What emotional sources of pain are you entertaining?
Ask God to reveal the aching emotional cycles in your life that are causing you pain and allow Him to heal your heart.

**Reference**

He heals the brokenhearted
And binds up their wounds.

– Psalm 147:3 (NKJV)

# Day 16: The Golden Rule

**Listen**

K. Michelle – How Many Times (2011)

**Read**

How much longer will you allow him to hurt you? You caught him lying or cheating. If he wasn't lying or cheating, he was misleading you. Perhaps he was withholding the truth, or lying by omission, which is still lying. He betrayed you! The evidence is in your face, but you take him back. As women, we are emotionally strong beings, some would say emotionally stronger than men. How many of you know a guy who was so emotionally struck by a woman that he became emotionally unavailable? In some cases, the result of men being players traces back to a woman who first hurt him. He has never healed. Yes, men shut down to the ideal of love as well.

In the book of Matthew, Peter asked Jesus, "how many times should I forgive?" (Matthew 18:21 NKJV).

Jesus responded, "Up to seventy times seven!" (Matthew 18:22 NKJV).

Jesus further shares the story of a wicked servant, who owed his master a debt (Matthew 18:23). The servant pleaded with his master and the master offered him loan forgiveness (Matthew 18:27). If only Sallie Mae would have the heart of this master! I digress.

Back to the story, the same servant went to his fellow servant and demanded repayment on a loan (Matthew 18:28). The fellow servant could not repay his debt, so the wicked servant sent him to jail (Matthew 18:30). When the master discovered the wicked servant's deeds, he sent the wicked servant to a tortuous fate until his debt was paid in full (Matthew 18:31-34).

Really think about this, if you betrayed that man the same as he did you, would he accept you back? Remember, some men don't handle emotional impact as well as we do. Would he accept you back knowing you may break his heart again? If the answer is no, think of this man as the wicked servant. He will not have mercy on you like the master. That means you condemn him to a tortuous fate until he pays his debt to you, right? It's not your job to throw that man in *jail*. God will handle that part. Your part is to forgive, but do not give him another chance to do the same thing again.

## Reference

And just as you want men to do to you, you also do to them likewise.
– Luke 6:31 (NKJV)

# Day 17: Second . . . Third . . . One Hundred Chances?

**Listen**

Alicia Keys feat. John Mayer – Lesson Learned (2007)

**Read**

You call your best friend to tell her, he doesn't deserve not another chance. Thinking a double negative will emphasize your point. You make a promise that this is the last time you will allow him to hurt you. Only to find yourself the next day calling your best friend again to convince her when you're really convincing yourself that he deserves *just* one more chance. This cycle continues until you look up one day and realize *just* one more chance has multiplied. Now that *one* chance has become a hundred chances. How does *just* one more chance multiply to a hundred chances?

Yesterday, we learned Jesus told us to forgive seventy-times seven, right (Matthew 18:22)? Yes, true, but in all seriousness, you can forgive him while still learning your own lesson. Every time you give him another chance, you're not forgiving yourself. You thought he would complete the perfect picture you painted in your mind. You thought he was *the one*, but now you must admit that you made a mistake. You played a role in your own repeated heartbreak.

Don't fret. There is good news. What's the good news here? You know the art of forgiveness. You can forgive yourself because you have already exhibited the ability to forgive him. Even if it takes falling for him seven or one hundred times, you *will* learn your lesson and forgive yourself.

## Reference

The godly may trip seven times, but they will get up again

But one disaster is enough to overthrow the wicked.

– Proverbs 24:16 (NLT)

# Day 18: To Have And To Hold?

**Listen**

Avant – Don't Take Your Love Away (2003)

**Read**

Don't be too quick to throw away love or friendships at the first sign of troubles. We already discussed how forgiving, but not learning your lesson, could cause you heartbreak. Now we have two extremes for comparison: being forgiving to a fault and not being forgiving at all, which is also a fault. Either extreme hurts *you* more than anyone else in the end.

If you dismiss every person in your life, you will find yourself on an island with a population of one, without the beautiful gift of fellowship. We will take a deeper dive into the importance of fellowship another day.

In the meantime, keep in mind, God gave us the gift of fellowship and no one is perfect. Jesus told us, the person with no sin should throw the first stone (John 8:7). There will be troubles, but know the difference between it's time to say goodbye and running away. What's the difference? You will recognize you're running away if times get tough and you interchange love for fear. Then, you proceed to throw up the deuces and exit stage left.

All people will make mistakes, including you, but how do you know when someone who erred is still worthy of your love? Simply ask God. Ask Him for His judgment in the Spirit. Pray for a discerning spirit. Then, discuss the fault with that person and receive his or her response. A part of learning to love and heal involves understanding that you gain freedom when you depend on God to lead you in every direction of your daily life.

**Reference**

If another believer sins against you, go privately and point out the offense. If the other person listens and confesses it, you have won that person back.

— Matthew 18:15 (NLT)

# Day 19: Play Ball!

**Listen**

Pink – Please Don't Leave Me (2008)

**Read**

I have been annoying, obnoxious, insulting, intrusive, and demeaning towards men. I have been known to jump to conclusions and take honest intentions out of context. There have been times where I've been running farther and farther into left field, when the ball hasn't even left home plate. Yet, there have been men who didn't strike me out at the first sign of a *ball*, in other words the first sign of trouble. These men may have enjoyed torture, or perhaps they just loved to play the game. Sometimes, to my surprise, these men would defy the rules of the game. I would find myself with three strikes, but he wouldn't strike me out.

Each time I would question, why he wouldn't leave me alone? My own insecurities and past situations were clearly dictating my interactions with new men. I was requesting chance after chance, but there are only so many recurrent apologies someone is willing to accept. Eventually, these men would end the game, thus striking me out. I had no foundational base to blame them.

*Single Ladies*, can you relate? We learned about being fearful of love, this is a well-illustrated example of interchanging fear with love. Although these men chose to remove themselves from our team, becoming free agents, God will never do this. Do not be afraid, He will never forsake you (Deuteronomy 31:6). No matter how many times you fail to indisputably slide into third base. God is the umpire of this game. If He says you're safe, you're safe. Don't be afraid to make it a home run in the first inning for the opportunity to love, or to live in your purpose. God has already secured a win for you, so walk in it with courage.

**Reference**

Be strong and of good courage, do not fear nor be afraid of them; for the Lord your God, He is the One who goes with you. He will not leave you nor forsake you.

– Deuteronomy 31:6 (NKJV)

## Day 20: Over the Mountains and Down the River!

**Listen**

Emeli Sandé – River (2012)

**Read**

If Jochebed never sealed her baby boy, Moses, in a basket and placed him in the Nile River (Exodus 2:3), what would have happened to Moses? If Jochebed never trusted God to lead her baby boy safely to the end of the river, would we have ever heard the story of Moses? Only God knows the answers to these questions. One thing is for sure. If Pharaoh had his premeditated way, Moses would still be in the Nile River; only he would be deceased in the river with all the other baby boys.

In the final moments of his river journey, God led baby Moses to Pharaoh's daughter and kept him safe (Exodus 2:5-10). Exactly how God guided baby Moses to safety, God will guide you down your own river. Your river is your path to healing. God is telling you, *follow Me*. I am the River! Once you learn to trust Him, you will find that He has already prepared a place for you at the end of the river. You can't swim? He won't allow you to drown. He'll be your life jacket. He'll go before you to make your yokes lighter. Consequently, *predestining* all things in your favor. Have faith and He'll give you the power to move mountains. He'll do the legwork for you.

All you have to do is trust Him through both your struggles and your peaceful moments. Follow Him! Follow the River!

**Reference**

"Do not be afraid or discouraged, for the Lord will personally go ahead of you. He will be with you; he will neither fail you nor abandon you."

– Deuteronomy 31:8 (NLT)

## Day 21: Snap Back

**Listen**

Ciara – Like A Boy (2006)

**Read**

You may have had those moments where you thought, *I would never treat him like he treats me.* Except, what if you did? What if you acted like a boy? What if you ignored him? Kept secrets. Cheated on him. Snapped on him without warning. You could *certainly* tell him you love him, but never mean it. You may end up as the suspect on an episode of a crime reality television show, but at least you'll get your point across, right? The answer is no. Don't retaliate. Recognize *who you are.* Don't change who you are for any man and certainly don't change your gender role. I don't care what year it is; don't switch up God's natural roles for men and women.

Once, I was discussing my trending heartbreaks with a guy friend. Hoping he could offer a man's perspective and shed some light on my situation, he suggested that I try something different.

I jokingly responded, "What? Like women?" Only it's not a joke for many of us. Some of us have seriously thought about it and this is not God's desire for us. Perhaps you've only been curious about venturing over to your neighbor's garden. Her flowers are plentiful and the grass looks greener, but don't do it. This is an abomination to God (Leviticus 20:13). Snap back, and ask God to remove that desire from your life. Replace that desire with a relationship amidst God. Build a *love affair* with God.

## Reference

For this reason God gave them up to vile passions. For even their women exchanged the natural use for what is against nature. Likewise also the men, leaving the natural use of the woman, burned in their lust for one another, men with men committing what is shameful, and receiving in themselves the penalty of their error which was due.

– Romans 1:26-27 (NKJV)

# Day 22: You *Tried* It!

**Listen**

Pink – Perfect (2010)

**Read**

"You *tried* it!" How many times have you thought this about that one person that constantly tries you? People will try you. It's inevitable. How will they try *it*? They will lie, cheat, or steal. People may lie to your face, cheat to get ahead with you, or steal your material belongings, but make up in your mind that no one steals your peace. I don't know any thieves who come back bearing your belongings as gifts. Consequently, there's no reason to beg, grovel, or cry. You have security in God. He is the best insurance plan money can't buy. The Lord will recover it all for you. Everything regarding you will be made perfect (Psalm 138:8).

People may attempt to negatively brand you. This is another way people may try you. The critics may try to ridicule you until you start to believe those negative critiques yourself. If people aren't trying you, maybe you're trying yourself. You may be your worst patronizing critic and not even realize it. *Single Ladies*, we are all human. We all make mistakes. Just because you made a wrong decision doesn't mean you are anything less than your God-given calling. God wants you to see you like He sees you–perfect. Perfect doesn't mean you are a god without any spot, blemish, or wrinkle. It simply means He created you perfectly in His image and He will never forsake His own perfect creation.

**Reference**

The Lord will perfect that which concerns me;

Your mercy, O Lord, endures forever;

Do not forsake the works of Your hands.

– Psalm 138:8 (NKJV)

## Day 23: Pick a Card, Any Card

**Listen**

Nicki Minaj – Freedom [Clean] (2012)

**Read**

Pick a card, any card. This is an abstract method for casting lots. The method people applied to distribute Jesus' garments before He died on the cross (Luke 23:34).

Before Jesus died, the people mocked and ridiculed Him, yet He still prayed for them, "Father, forgive them, for they do not know what they do" (Luke 23:34 NKJV).

In a previous job, I worked closely with my customer, being he had oversight in our daily process. One particular day, he had a concern external to my scope of work, and I contacted the senior project lead. The customer and the project lead engaged in a discussion while I dismissed myself to pursue my other duties. The next day, I was on vacation. Upon my return, a colleague approached me with astonishment. He couldn't believe that I arrogantly confronted the customer. I thought this must be a mistake; perhaps, everyone was confusing me with the senior project lead. As the day went on, more rumors ensued, not only was I arrogant, I insulted the customer. Until finally the project lead shared the real story. The customer lied, and spread the rumors about me. I racked my brain to justify why he would do such a thing. Then, I recalled a couple weeks ago when I gracefully declined his lunch invitation.

Remember, *Single Ladies*, the unbelievers of the world do not acknowledge Jesus for dying on the cross for their sins. If they did, they would not be of the world. Truth is, they may not acknowledge you either. If they do, it may only be to disrespect you, or like in my case, spread rumors about you. Why would they do this? The customer did not spread rumors only because I declined his offer. There's a deeper reasoning. He honestly could have picked any other reason out of a black top hat, and the deeper reasoning would still stand. On the outside, you and the world may look similar. You are indeed a human being like them, and you bleed red like them, but on the inside you're different than the world. God has chosen you (John 15:16). He set you apart from the world and the Holy Spirit resides in you. For this reason, like Jesus, men may mock and ridicule you too. They may even attempt to scam you with card tricks. Understand the world hated Jesus without a cause (John 15:18). Therefore, don't find yourself alarmed, when the world hates you with *cause*. Find comfort in that you are not alone. Jesus knows how you feel. Like Jesus, forgive them.

**Reference**

"If the world hates you, you know that it hated Me before it hated you. If you were of the world, the world would love its own. Yet because you are not of the world, but I chose you out of the world, therefore the world hates you. Remember the word that I said to you, 'A servant is not greater than his master.' If they persecuted Me, they will also persecute you. If they kept My word, they will keep yours also."

– John 15:18-20 (NKJV)

## Day 24: An Eye For An Eye

**Listen**

Nick Jonas – Jealous [Clean] (2014)

**Read**

Happiness is an abode where you do not envy another person's life, blessings, talents, or visions. Understand you have your own beautiful attributes to share with the world. On the other hand, do not allow someone's envy for your possessions to steal your joy. Situations may make you angry, but do not sin (Ephesians 4:26). Neither jealousy, nor wrath should cause you to sin (Ephesians 4:26). Do not allow other women hovering over a man you're dating to cause jealousy to resonate in you. Instead, turn the other cheek (Matthew 5:39). If he's the man for you, those temptations won't consume him.

Recall yesterday's anecdote with my customer, who fabricated a story about me. He was upset that I wouldn't go out to lunch with him, so he retaliated. After the incident, I wondered if I should confront him, ultimately deciding I wouldn't give him another opportunity to spread more rumors. I passed him in the hallway and greeted him with a hello. Then, overpoweringly followed my greeting with an evil look. I asked God for forgiveness right then and there. Although this man attempted to destroy my character, I should mirror Jesus by turning the other cheek. I realized I should pray for him, he doesn't realize his actions. Our spiritual fight is against powers and principalities, not flesh and blood (Ephesians 6:12). Jesus instructed us not to fight wicked people (Matthew 5:39).

Understand the meaning of turning the other cheek. It doesn't mean someone steals the tires off your car, so you go out looking for the criminal hoping you can give them your entire car. Perhaps the most applicative example involves a man who cheats on his wife for years, and then divorces his wife. She can't afford one of the best lawyers; while her husband hires the best lawyer money can buy. The wife's lawyer somehow manages a preliminary settlement offer for the house, the car, and the boat. Yet, the woman *turns the other cheek* declining it all. Instead, she seeks God to provide all her needs, and forgives her husband. God will bless this woman for her obedience as He will bless you in your own situation for your obedience in turning the other cheek.

## Reference

"You have heard that it was said, 'An eye for an eye and a tooth for a tooth.' But I tell you not to resist an evil person. But whoever slaps you on your right cheek, turn the other to him also. If anyone wants to sue you and take away your tunic, let him have your cloak also. And whoever compels you to go one mile, go with him two. Give to him who asks you, and from him who wants to borrow from you do not turn away."

– Matthew 5:38-42 (NKJV)

# Day 25: Déjà Vu

**Listen**

Deitrick Haddon's LXW (League of Xtraordinary Worshippers) –
Healing Virtue Flow (2014)

**Read**

If you desire inward healing, pray for it, and believe you will receive
healing. If you desire physical healing, pray for it, and believe you will
receive healing. This is not a misprint, nor is this a typo. No, you
didn't just have déjà vu, and it wasn't just your imagination. These
very similar affirmations were written twice for a reason. *Single Ladies*,
make your requests known to God, ask for it, and then declare it until
you receive it. A man may become annoyed when you repeatedly ask
21 questions, but God is never annoyed when you remind Him of
His promises for your life. If you have to say it, or write it down
twice, God welcomes it (1 Thessalonians 5:16-17). In fact, the Holy
Bible describes how we should pray. We should come humbly before
God and make our requests known to God (Philippians 4:6).

Now, it's a different story if you're asking for something and
God already responded, *No.* Let's say, you ask God to bring a toxic
ex-boyfriend back into your life, but God's response is no. Trust that
God knows what's best for you.

Love, healing, freedom, and purpose are promises of God.
Request these promises of God. Then, begin to thank God for

fulfilling those promises in advance. Whatever you desire and whatever you pray, pray for it earnestly, and without wavering or doubting. Do you desire healing by His stripes (Isaiah 53:5)? Do you desire inward healing? Guess what, *Single Ladies*? You got it! You are healed!

**Reference**

But He was wounded for our transgressions,

He was bruised for our iniquities;

The chastisement for our peace was upon Him,

And by His stripes we are healed.

– Isaiah 53:5 (NKJV)

# Day 26: Catch 22

**Listen**

Kirk Franklin – Without You (2005)

**Read**

Have you ever looked around you and thought this can't be life? You're flying high, and then you're down. Your daily encounters feel like an act, and no matter how hard you try, nothing seems to go your way. Life feels like a Catch 22. You have goals. You have desires, but the more you attempt to accomplish them, it appears the less attainable those desires become. You think you found the job or the man of your dreams, but then you wake up and realize that the experience was just that–a dream, not reality. It's not always easy picking yourself back up, dusting yourself off, and pushing along, but you have the capability. You have the Lord on your side and He is your strength! Wait on the Lord: be of good courage (Psalm 27:14 NKJV).

Despite your surroundings, commit to being genuine. Commit to being authentic. In the end you will win, keep your focus on God and you will prevail! You will no longer play the crying game. Your heart will heal. Your mind will refocus, and you'll have new joys everlasting!

**Reference**

But those who trust in the Lord will find new strength.

They will soar high on wings like eagles.

They will run and not grow weary.

They will walk and not faint.

– Isaiah 40:31 (NLT)

## Day 27: Non-Value Added

**Listen**

Leona Lewis – Better In Time (2007)

**Read**

What is a day? 24 hours, which equals 1,440 minutes, which equals 86,400 seconds. What is a year? 52 weeks, which equals 365 days, which equals 8,760 hours, which equals 525,600 minutes, which equals 31,536,000 seconds. That's a mouthful, but does this establish perspective on your time value? Your time is precious and you can never purchase any additional time.

Healing takes time, but how much of your valuable time will you spend? When you take days, months, or years to heal, are you cognizant of the amount of time you are spending? How much of that time is not value added to your healing process? Anything that doesn't add value is a waste, so how can you remove the waste?

When you're not ready to move on from the source of your pain, attempting to accept healing situates you in an uncomfortable position. For instance, when you're torn between staying in love with a guy, who is not loving you genuinely, and leaving him alone. You're conflicted between being honest with yourself and misleading yourself. This is wasteful, and it clocks time.

When you are torn, you're holding onto some inkling that he will eventually desire to be with you whole-heartedly, not halfheartedly like before. This is a time waster because you're fearful of progressing to the next step in your life. You think, if I fall out of love with him and he has a change of heart, I might miss out on an opportunity with him all together. He'll come back loving you, but you'll no longer feel the same. You have either reached complete healing, or God forbid found another scandalous man. At least, this is your rationalization.

After some time has passed, and he comes back wholeheartedly desiring you, you'll be fearfully left wondering, what if? What if you had stayed in love with him all this time? The next step would have been an engagement, and then you would be on the road to marital bliss. There would be no more *searching*–I mean waiting, of course, and no more hoping you would receive love. If it makes you feel better, or if it helps you heal; be confident in this, if he is meant to come back to you, the feelings will still be there as if he never left. This doesn't mean you should bank on this. Instead, operate with *security*, if it's meant to be it will be. No time apart will change that. It doesn't hurt for you to give up on loving him for now. You wouldn't lose anything. If you're supposed to let go for good, you'll gain so much more; you'll gain healing without wasting valuable time.

We are guilty of aimlessly telling ourselves, *if it is meant to be it will be*, but not really accepting it. Thinking that dating other men signifies we moved on, and we're not waiting for the last guy to figure things out on his end; knowing very well that we have not healed from the past situation, or maybe even situations. Don't do that to yourself. Don't jump into the dating pool, a relationship, or a marriage without healing first. Your insecurities will be evident and your pain will be vibrant. Heal first. Take time to heal without the waste or distractions. Healing and time makes things better; it helps you lose sight of the past and live freely in your future. Learn to live in complete freedom. Where do you find freedom? Freedom is found in the Spirit of the Lord (2 Corinthians 3:17).

**Reference**

For the Lord is the Spirit, and wherever the Spirit of the Lord is, there is freedom.

– 2 Corinthians 3:17 (NLT)

# Commandment #3

# Freedom

Thou shall live in unadulterated freedom, freedom from every past thing and situation.

# Day 28: Only God Can Judge Me

**Listen**

Chris Brown – Don't Judge Me (2012)

**Read**

*Only God Can Judge Me* is an expression tattooed on the body, written on walls, shouted on the mountaintops, and even *hashtagged* on social media. If this is the case, then why do we yet appoint ourselves as judge? The irony is a court appointed judge protects and defends liberty; but those not appointed as judge, gain liberty when they do not judge. You receive merciful judgment from God when you do not judge others. You also gain freedom. Instead of focusing on others' faults, accept accountability, transform yourself, and gain freedom from your own faults.

Jesus asked, "Why worry about a speck in your friend's eye when you have a log in your own?" (Matthew 7:3 NLT).

Picture yourself at the gym with a friend. You both walk toward the cardio equipment and decide to exercise on automated stationary bicycles. You program your bike settings for the manual workout consisting of a straight, flat course with zero resistance. You notice your friend inputs the same settings. You look over at your friend, thinking she needs this workout more than you.

Consequently, you suggest she try one of the hill setting workouts. Only you failed to look at yourself in the mirror lately. You need the gym just as much, if not more, than your friend. Understand that the same intensity you exert to judge someone else applies toward you. That effort is better exerted evolving yourself. Why not exercise those *personal growth* muscles, instead of exercising your self-appointment as judge pro tem? Understand when you gain knowledge, God holds you accountable of that newfound knowledge. At the appointed time, we will each give an account of our actions to God (Romans 14:12).

If only God is the Judge, when do people have the authority to judge? Solomon was a wise judge, but we must recall the source of Solomon's wisdom (1 Kings 3). Solomon received his appointment to judge from the Lord (1 Kings 3:11). Solomon asked God for His wisdom to govern people (1 Kings 3:9). When God appoints you to judge, judge in the Holy Spirit with wisdom and love.

**Reference**

Do not judge others, and you will not be judged. For you will be treated as you treat others. The standard you use in judging is the standard by which you will be judged.

– Matthew 7:1-2 (NLT)

# Day 29: Spring Forward, Fall Back

**Listen**

Chrisette Michele – Blame It On Me (2009)

**Read**

Learning when to say goodbye in a toxic or stunted relationship is an aptitude. Yes, he had his faults, but it takes a level of maturity to take responsibility for your own actions. Admitting fault and letting go is not a weakness.

Our society encourages us to never quit. You do anything necessary to race through the finish line, even if you have to bleed sweat and tears in order to overcome life's challenges. Only life is not a race, the woman who runs the fastest to her college degree, down the wedding aisle, or to a house with two children and a dog, all surrounded with a white picket fence, is not prized the winner. The woman, who gains wisdom, but loses guilt, the woman who keeps humility, but throws away arrogance; she is the woman who wins. The woman, who figuratively speaking, throws away a man she knows is not meant for her but keeps her relationship with God, she wins! She wins because she has peace and understanding. She knows that there is a season for everything and that each season happens in God's perfect timing. No need for daylight savings time. This woman *springs* into her *freedom* because she learned to *fall* back from her past.

**Reference**

A time to gain,

And a time to lose;

A time to keep,

And a time to throw away

– Ecclesiastes 3:6 (NKJV)

# Day 30: Road to Freedom

**Listen**

Usher – Confessions Part II (2004)

**Read**

Confessing your wrongs is never easy. When we confess our indiscretions, we should confess not just to the one we wronged (James 5:16), but also to God (1 John 1:9). You may admit it is already hard enough to confess to just one person. Why should we confess to one another and God?

Understand this, our personal freedom lies in the act of confessing. Have you ever been practically placed under oath on the Bible to keep a secret, but you shared the secret anyway? Maybe you justified telling the secret because you were confident the person you told wouldn't share it with anyone else, or maybe the person didn't know the individuals involved in the secret. Plus everyone knows the unwritten rule: when I promise not to tell a secret to *anyone*, my best friend doesn't count. Whatsoever the reasoning, you knew one thing for a fact, if you didn't share that juicy secret with someone, you would have inevitably exploded!

What if confessing your sins resembled the desire you had to share that secret? When you confess to God, you are no longer bound to the sins you committed. Jesus Christ already served as

74

atonement when He died on the cross to save all of us from our sins. Confession is His gift to us. Embrace this beautiful gift of freedom.

### Reference

If we confess our sins, He is faithful and just to forgive us our sins and to cleanse us from all unrighteousness.

·— 1 John 1:9 (NKJV)

## Day 31: Life's Basic Essentials

**Listen**

Jazmine Sullivan – Need U Bad (2008)

**Read**

You need him bad, but how bad do you need God? It should be far greater than you need him, but if you're saying you need him as bad as you need food, breath, life, and water, what else is left to need of God?

Be careful not to put any man before God. God warns us of doing so. Even when you marry, your husband should not take the place of God. We understand our God is a jealous God (Exodus 34:14). Just think about what people do when they become jealous. They may be able to contain that jealousy for a while, but eventually it seeps out and they react. God is no different. He will eventually react and you will see that very person, or even thing you put before Him demoted or removed from your life.

Well, why would God do this? He is a just and forgiving God. This is true. However, scary as it may sound, when you say you need a man to breathe or to live, you're subconsciously saying you no longer need God and that man becomes your *god*. God is the ultimate provider. He created all things, so think about it, whom do you really need badly? Do you need the all-knowing provider, or man, who is purely a creation of God?

**Reference**

For you shall worship no other god, for the Lord, whose name is Jealous, is a jealous God.

– Exodus 34:14 (NKJV)

# Day 32: Clueless?

**Listen**

Aaliyah – Don't Know What To Tell Ya (2003)

**Read**

Let's be clear, confusion is not of God (1 Corinthians 14:33). If you're going back and forth with a man and he doesn't know if he wants to be lovers or friends, then pack up your bags and keep it moving. No questions asked. It's not worth the drama and it's not worth the stress. Otherwise, you're inflicting a self-induced headache, and for no good reason.

Before you pack up your bags and hit the road, as a woman you just have to ask the question: How do you know if a man sees you as a wife, or a friend? The answer: His actions will show you. God calls this the fruit of a man. We'll talk more about this fruit another day. Back to the matter at hand, you shouldn't have to guess, play 21 questions, follow the breadcrumbs, or play the game of clue to get his answer. It should be clear! If he is flip-flopping or going back and forth, the unfortunate truth is, he may not see you as a wife. A man should have some inkling that he desires you as a wife and should treat you as such. I know it's hard to accept. I've played the game and danced in circles with men, but there comes a time when you stop pretending that you're naïve and accept reality. You're not clueless, nor are you Cher Horowitz. Maybe you pretend for fear of being alone, but all that energy you're spending wastefully on men can be invested in God.

## Reference

For God is not *the author* of confusion but of peace, as in all the churches of the saints.

– 1 Corinthians 14:33 (NKJV)

# Day 33: E=t

**Listen**

Keri Hilson – Energy (2009)

**Read**

*E=t;* in other words, wasted *Energy* equates to *time* that you will never get back!

If you're seeing, talking to, communicating, dating, friends with benefits, in a courtship, relationship, or even a *situationship*, with a man . . . (I believe that covers most descriptions), and you know he's not potential husband material; **it's not worth your energy**. If he doesn't see you as a potential wife, **he's not worth your energy**. Do yourself a favor, grab your visual scissors, and cut him out of your life.

As *Single Ladies*, we may get lonely, but we shouldn't waste precious energy on a man with no courtship potential. Sometimes it's not even courtship that we desire. Sometimes, we just desire a good conversation, and not with our female best friend. We want to talk to a man. Believe me, I understand. However, if you can honestly admit to yourself that you're wasting energy on any man that leads to no future, redirect your energy, and spend that time with God. As God's *Single Ladies,* we shouldn't be dating any man, if we don't *first* have our relationship in order with God.

Imagine yourself *finally* walking down the aisle, dressed in all white, or cream–whatever works for you. Remember, you dreamed of this day since you were a little girl. You're a bride! Finally, a bride, and staring at the other end of the aisle is your groom–Jesus Christ. That's the vision of marriage God desires for you as a single woman. That doesn't mean you're running around telling every man you meet that you don't need a husband because you're married to Jesus. It just means that you are first and foremost concerned with investing your energy wisely on your love affair with your Savior, Jesus Christ. Be selective when determining who deserves your energy. After all, you can't pay any amount of money to get that time back, so why waste it?

**Reference**

. . . The unmarried woman cares about the things of the Lord, that she may be holy both in body and in spirit. But she who is married cares about the things of the world—how she may please her husband.

– 1 Corinthians 7:34 (NKJV)

# Day 34: What My Eyes See

**Listen**

Rihanna – Do Ya Thang (2011)

**Read**

You want to be the cool chick. The one who doesn't sweat about the *little stuff*, so you accept him with all his lies and cheating. Nobody's perfect, right? Be honest with yourself. Do you really want a man who stares down and *gasses up* every woman he sees? Do you want a man who flirts with every woman he finds attractive? Of course any red-blooded man will take a glance at a beautiful woman, it's in his nature, but he shouldn't lust after every beautiful woman. If you noticed this conduct during the dating phase, as *Single Ladies* you shouldn't be wasting your energy. If he behaves in this manner now, how do you think he'll act if you two were married? He may very well continue to feed that lustful spirit. Instead of a man lusting over the flesh, how about consider dating a man lusting over the Spirit of God?

Men are not the only ones guilty of feeding lust. We are guilty too. Learn to put your lust in check using the Spirit (Romans 8:13-14). Tomorrow isn't promised; pray that your flesh die daily (Romans 8:13-14), so you may be positively minded today, and consequently live in God's forever.

**Reference**

For all that is in the world—the lust of the flesh, the lust of the eyes, and the pride of life—is not of the Father but is of the world. And the world is passing away, and the lust of it; but he who does the will of God abides forever.

– 1 John 2:16-17 (NKJV)

# Day 35: Don't be a Fool!

**Listen**

Cee Lo Green feat. Melanie Fiona – Fool For You (2011)

**Read**

Don't be a fool for anyone. Claiming to be a fool makes you exactly that. Be careful of the things you speak out of your mouth. We will further discuss the reasons why another day. Until then, realize that foolish behavior only leads you down the road to destruction, the wrong road (Ecclesiastes 10:2). Instead follow the road of wisdom; doing so is a direct reflection of self-love (Proverbs 19:8). With intention and honesty, serve God; this is the wise thing to do.

Understand just because you choose wisdom, it doesn't mean your road will be easier. However, it does mean that in the end, if you don't give up, you will obtain the ultimate reward of everlasting life (Galatians 6:9, Romans 6:23). This is a reward God gifts to those who diligently seek Him and His wisdom. Those who are wise will go through trials and tribulations, but understand you will have the victory. You possess wisdom in understanding that Jesus gives you the strength to overcome.

**Reference**

A wise person chooses the right road;

a fool takes the wrong one.

– Ecclesiastes 10:2 (NLT)

# Day 36: Lost and Found

**Listen**

Mary J. Blige – Take Me As I Am (2005)

**Read**

Over the years, I've learned the importance of mentorship. I seek women mentors who have a knowledge base that I do not possess. I seek women mentors who are in a position that I would like to achieve. I surround myself with women who hold greater wisdom than my own because these women can save me from making some common mistakes. You can practice this exercise as well. It doesn't mean you'll gain that woman's 20 or 30 years of wisdom in one hour, but you will gain more than you formerly possessed. The best insight I have received concerning the lifespan of womanhood is that as you pick up years, you learn to drop down baggage. You do not need to carry every frivolous object with you to your every destination. This is wisdom and you find peace in this concept of wisdom.

Lacking the wisdom to decipher through life's chaos can make you feel like a lost sheep without a shepherd. Take comfort in the fact that with years comes the wisdom to decipher that every issue is not worth your concern or headache. As you gain wisdom, use those decoding skills to decipher through the noise of this world and hear God's voice. Learn to listen for God's voice, receive His voice, and follow His voice (John 10:27). This is what God desires for you. God will rejoice because you have been found (Luke 15:6). You are no longer a lost sheep because you follow G-O-D.

## Reference

My sheep hear My voice, and I know them, and they follow Me.

– John 10:27 (NKJV)

## Day 37: Let Them Eat Cake?

**Listen**

Trey Songz – Cake (2014)

**Read**

I'm talking to my *Single Ladies* here, so hear this: your cake should never be on the menu. Giving away your cake is **never** what you're supposed to do. Your body is a precious gift on loan to you by God. Think about this. If you apply for a school loan, would you blow the funds on any and everything, but school? Well, if you did, how would you pay for school?

If you're giving your cake away, you take from your own body, leaving you with little to no remaining portions for your body's true intention. Your body is intended as the Lord's temple, where the Holy Spirit should dwell (1 Corinthians 6:19). Even if you have given slices of your cake away, God can redeem you. Understand that your cake doesn't belong on an uncovered cake stand for any man who is not your husband. Believe me, I know it's not easy refraining. After all, even edible cake is delicious. Although you may feel tempted to share your delicious red velvet cake with a man, you understand your cake is so good that you should savor it for your husband who is worthy of receiving a slice of your cake. Save your cake, *Single Ladies*!

**Reference**

Run from sexual sin! No other sin so clearly affects the body as this one does. For sexual immorality is a sin against your own body.

– 1 Corinthians 6:18 (NLT)

## Day 38: God's Property

**Listen**

Trin-i-tee 5:7 – My Body (1999)


**Read**

You know your cake is not on the menu, but how do you make up in your mind that celibacy is the way you will live your life? Not just that, how do you even know if celibacy is really the way you *want* to live your life? Truth is, sex is all around you. You hear about it in songs on the radio, you see it on the television, and you may even talk about it over dinner with your friends. I do not have an easy answer for you, but I will share this. When you begin to seek God in all aspects of your life, your thoughts on sex will begin to line up with God's will. Even if you make the attempt to ask God into your life, but still try to keep God out of your sex life, you will find that your thoughts on the subject will have no choice but to become elevated.

Here are a few tips on pursuing a life of celibacy. Seek ways to immerse yourself in the Lord. Ask for forgiveness for sinning against your own body. Ask for a heart's desire to serve God in all His truths. Pray for the will to conduct yourself in a manner that is a reflection of His holiness. Finally, pray for a realization of your true value. If you need to meditate on today's song or make it your anthem, do it. Do whatever you have to do to stay focused on the goal. You are God's Property, *Single Ladies*, and your body is too!

**Reference**

Don't you realize that your body is the temple of the Holy Spirit, who lives in you and was given to you by God? You do not belong to yourself, for God bought you with a high price. So you must honor God with your body.

– 1 Corinthians 6:20 (NLT)

# Day 39: What's Your Superpower?

**Listen**

Chris Brown feat. Keri Hilson – Superhuman (2007)

**Read**

Choose a superpower, whichever one you like. Seriously, pick one. Which did you choose? Flying, super strength, *spidey* senses, or invisibility? Would you like to know which one I chose? Jesus Christ's superpower. That's right, Jesus' superpower. Do you know why? He is the ultimate superhero with one of the greatest superpowers. He is the only superhero ever to actually save the world. He has a perfect track record! What other superhero can claim that? He's also the only superhero with the ability to transfer power, real supernatural power! I understand that when I have Jesus in my life, I am equipped to overcome anything! Whether it's sickness, drama, or heartbreak, we are all more than overcomers because we have Jesus!

His supernatural power is transferable and essential to helping you get through any trial and any tribulation. The enemy knows you have a greater purpose and because of this the enemy attacks you. He attacks you with sickness, drama, and especially heartbreak to attempt to destroy you. Through Jesus, you have the strength to defeat the enemy in a spiritual battle. Not only will you defeat the enemy, but your testimony, your story, and your elevation will be used for God's glory to save other people who have experienced similar struggles. Tap into Jesus' supernatural power in order to overcome your own challenges and save yourself. Don't keep your superpower all to yourself, go out and save the world for God!

**Reference**

I can do all things through Christ who strengthens me.

– Philippians 4:13 (NKJV)

# Day 40: Myth Buster

**Listen**

Estelle – Conqueror (2015)

**Read**

The rumors you heard are true. We are in a spiritual battle. Principalities and powers are surrounding and wrestling against us (Ephesians 6:12). Be confident in this fact, Jesus conquered the grave so that you may have victory over all of life's battles (1 Corinthians 15:57). God gave you a vision, be confident in your vision. Believe that you have the strength through Jesus Christ and the equipment inside of you to accomplish it! You can make that vision a reality.

Many times, the enemy uses the very desire you long for the most to distract you. You may desire a husband so the enemy distracts you with tall, dark, and handsome men, none of whom is your God-ordained husband. The enemy feeds on your desire because he believes you will falter and fail if he keeps you distracted. He attempts to overcome you through feeding you this myth in an attempt to keep this truth secret from you.

Myth: You are a conqueror.

Truth: You are **more** than a conqueror (Romans 8:37).

When this secret becomes an apparent truth, the enemy knows *you* will have the victory. This truth becomes your footstool. You don't repay good for evil. You have the victory because you choose not to retaliate against the principalities and powers! Now that you know the secret, what will you do with it? Thank God for this wisdom and understanding, and then disperse into the world. Be more than a conqueror; encounter your vision with this truth!

**Reference**

Yet in all these things we are more than conquerors through Him who loved us. For I am persuaded that neither death nor life, nor angels nor principalities nor powers, nor things present nor things to come, nor height nor depth, nor any other created thing, shall be able to separate us from the love of God which is in Christ Jesus our Lord.

– Romans 8:37-39 (NKJV)

## Day 41: Gaze Into My Crystal Ball

**Listen**

John Legend and Common – Glory (2014)

**Read**

Clairvoyance, crystal balls, tarot cards, telepathy, false prophets . . . don't allow any such mechanism to distract you with your own future. We know the enemy plays on our desires. He uses them as a weapon, hoping for spoils of war. Yes, you can dream about the future, but don't allow those desires to consume you. Be proactive and prepare for the attack. You prepare for the attack through focusing on God's present. Focus on His plan for you right now. Maybe that plan includes starting a non-profit, leading a youth group, or evangelizing in another country. Whatever it is, focus on those God-given ordinations.

The makings of this world can serve as a distraction to you as well. Your local news is flooded with senseless acts of violence, wars, and attacks. Of course, you should never live in ignorance. Be attentive, but do not be consumed. Don't allow yourself to become overly dismayed over the things you see in the world. Only God knows the end, but He gives believers a sneak peek. He promises that His glory will prevail in the end (Matthew 24:6, Matthew 24:14). Until that day comes, engulf yourself in God and any distractions used as a weapon can't devour you. Keep your eyes on the Lord!

**Reference**

And you will hear of wars and rumors of wars. See that you are not troubled; for all these things must come to pass, but the end is not yet.

– Matthew 24:6 (NKJV)

## Day 42: First Time and Last Time

**Listen**

Big Sean feat. Chris Brown – My Last (2011)

**Read**

God speaks. God speaks through His word and He even speaks through other people.

My friend was preparing for his first international business assignment in the Middle East.

We were discussing his upcoming trip, when I asked, "Are you ready for your trip?"

He responded, "I'm treating this trip as if it's my last time in business class."

At first glance, I misinterpreted his words, thinking he was declaring this wouldn't be his last time traveling internationally in business class. I departed on a tangent about how it's great that he looks at this opportunity as just the beginning of his business class experiences. Then, I realized that's not what he anticipated at all. He expected just the opposite and he was right. He was acknowledging this opportunity as his *first time and last time.* Tomorrow is not promised. I'm confident that I'm not the only one who loses sight of the promise that another day on this Earth *is not* promised (Proverbs 27:1). Be like my friend; learn to live each day to its fullest. Be humble as you welcome each opportunity provided to you.

Think about applying this learned concept to another dimension. Each waking morning of your life, you have another opportunity to accept Jesus Christ and live your life fulfilling His purpose. Only tomorrow morning on this Earth is not promised. Understanding this fact, accept God's will for your life with today's morning breath. Your guarantee of *eternal* life depends on it.

## Reference

Do not boast about tomorrow,

For you do not know what a day may bring forth.

– Proverbs 27:1 (NKJV)

## Day 43: Guilty Until Proven Innocent

**Listen**

Aaliyah – If Your Girl Only Knew (1996)

**Read**

Be honest. Tell me, have you ever hoped he would break it off with her and come running to you? If you're honest, you'll admit you *photobombed* the picture for this very prospect. Just for the possibility of having your presence requested in the picture instead of forced. You stick around for even the slightest chance of him claiming you as his own. You think about showing her text messages and the timestamp on the recent call log. It's not enough to present the frequency of the calls. The timestamp supports your evidence. The evidence showing that he calls you in all hours of the night. You think to yourself if he makes just one wrong move, you might not hesitate to prove to her that you exist in his world too. Then, *all* would be right in the world.

You refrain from this temptation, right? You are the bigger woman so you won't allow yourself to stoop that low. Since we're being honest, let's admit he may have taken you out of your character on one or two occasions. You succumbed to temptation, but you don't usually do this, and you *never* give into petty behavior.

Perhaps you're evaluating the scenario and it describes your character; you're the woman who reacts to situations without any filter. *Single Ladies,* you no longer have to be that woman. Just don't do it. You are bigger than this situation and you don't need to wrap yourself up in a man who is wrapped up in another woman.

Yes, you may have more perception into his web of lies than she does, but that doesn't place you any more ahead in this race. You may start to attack her as a woman. You conduct *a paralegal investigation on the girl,* which really translates to you stalking her social media page for clues. Thus leading to the question, *why isn't her female intuition kicking in?* You just knew there was something suspicious about him and badgered him about it. Yes, you questioned him, and you got your answer. Either the answer you didn't want to hear, or another set of his lies. Only you're smart and you read through those lies.

How do I know you did all this? I'll testify: I'm not innocent and I have been guilty of this offense. I've been that *girl,* keyword being girl, not woman. A woman recognizes that a female's intuition is really God-given discernment, serving as a warning for you. Instead of dwelling on how she's crazy or clueless, do yourself a favor and get off those unbalanced scales. As much as you like to think it's balanced, it's not. You're in a scalene love triangle and you're getting the shorter end of the triangle. In all actuality, you never know, it may be a love trapezoid, or even a love pentagon. Do you really want to find out for sure? He is not worth your character. Save yourself the trouble and heed your spirit of discernment.

**Reference**

And do not be conformed to this world, but be transformed by the renewing of your mind, that you may prove what is that good and acceptable and perfect will of God.

– Romans 12:2 (NKJV)

# Day 44: The Doctor Is In

**Listen**

Gnarls Barkley – Crazy (2006)

**Read**

There was a time when I self-diagnosed myself as a hypochondriac. I had sickness. I had disease. I had mental instability. I was depressed. Thank God, none of which was true. I just made all the symptoms up in my mind and any medical website or blog I could find to support my diagnosis was fair game.

You may hear people say, "You are what you eat." Well, you are also what you think and what you speak. Start speaking, "I'm crazy," and you may just start doing crazy things. We already discussed how claiming to be a fool makes you exactly that. The same applies to any other negative thing you speak. Start speaking, "No man will ever marry me," and you may just be setting yourself up for failure. Instead, begin speaking on all your delightful and desirable qualities. Speak confidently as you self-recite this scripture: *There are many virtuous and capable women in the world, but I surpass them all* (Proverbs 31:29 NLT).

You may ask how did I overcome my self-diagnosis? I got a second opinion from the doctor of doctors–God. He told me the true diagnosis for my condition was the enemy. The enemy attempted to use a self-diagnosis to take control of my mind with the intent to commit me. If you allow the enemy, he'll attempt to take control of your mind. He doesn't want you to inherit the promises of God. The enemy knows once he has possession of your mind, he can take your life too. Always be mindful of the things that you speak out of your mouth. Don't let the enemy commit you, speak freedom and live free!

## Reference

Death and life are in the power of the tongue,

And those who love it will eat its fruit.

– Proverbs 18:21 (NKJV)

# Day 45: Fight Night

## Listen

Lauryn Hill – Lost Ones (1998)


## Read

It's fight night, no Vegas. Your name isn't displayed in flashing lights. At first appearance, you may appear to be the underdog. Your opponent has fallen angels and demons in his corner. For you, there's no *money team*, but you do have an entourage. Three to be exact–the Father, the Son, and the Holy Spirit. The Holy Trinity is all you need on your team.

In life's fight, you may feel like your career, your children, or your college education are the only bragging rights on your boxing record, but not true. You have an amazing Trainer in your corner! Your opponent is cunning and swift. He is in the ring hoping for a knock out, but to his dismay, he only won one round. Remember your Trainer's teachings. Be attentive. You recognize your opponent's boxing style and technique. He attacks your weaknesses. Therefore, use this knowledge for your strength. Curve your weaknesses with God's strength. You may have lost this bout, but you have up to 11 more rounds remaining. You're a winner! Don't dwell on that one lost round, you have won countless fights in the past and you will win again!

**Reference**

Be sober, be vigilant; because your adversary the devil walks about like a roaring lion, seeking whom he may devour.

– 1 Peter 5:8 (NKJV)

# Day 46: It's D-Day!

**Listen**

Ne-Yo – Forever Now (2012)

**Read**

It's been a long and frustrating couple of weeks. You have argued, stressed, and wrestled. Now, the verdict is in. It's settled; your relationship is over. What will you do now? It's the end of your relationship and it's the end of your world forever. Wrong! When you reach the end of a relationship, it's certainly not the end of your world. It's D-Day! You heard me right, it is just D-Day! The day you change the course of this war. We all have the potential to become so consumed with our relationship and with him, that we may lose sight of the commander in this war. The commander is the One from whom you take your orders. It's quite obvious the commander-in-chief of this war is God.

He has entrusted you to lead a special operation. An operation that will change the course of any forthcoming battle you fight. Embrace your D-Day, it will make you a stronger woman of God and will prepare you for His marvelous glory.

Troubles don't last always. Thank God! Our present battles may seem like small victories, but those small battles amount to achieving the long-term mission. Thus, declaring you the winner of eternal freedom. This is the prize we will receive if we fight this fight under the direction of our commander-in-chief, GOD.

## Reference

For our present troubles are small and won't last very long. Yet they produce for us a glory that vastly outweighs them and will last forever!

– 2 Corinthians 4:17 (NLT)

## Day 47: Last in, First Out

**Listen**

Yolanda Adams – The Battle Is Not Yours (1996)

**Read**

You learned that God is the commander-in-chief of this war. *Single Ladies*, you are in God's army, but that doesn't mean you will win every battle you fight. You may lose a battle, but not the war. There are some steps you can follow to reduce the possibility of losing a battle.

1. Have faith that God will finish what He promised you. Sow faith. "You don't have enough faith," Jesus told them. "I tell you the truth, if you had faith even as small as a mustard seed, you could say to this mountain, *move from here to there*, and it would move. Nothing would be impossible" (Matthew 17:20 NLT).

2. Claim your authority.

"No weapon formed against you shall prosper,

And every tongue *which* rises against you in judgment

You shall condemn.

This *is* the heritage of the servants of the Lord,

And their righteousness *is* from Me,

Says the Lord" (Isaiah 54:17 NKJV).

109

3. Understand order does not matter. Recall the landowner who paid the laborers, who worked all day, the same amount as the laborers who worked only an hour (Matthew 20:8-14). *Single Ladies*, you have been chosen. You may not be the first to battle this particular foe, but recognize *the last will be first, and the first last. For many are called, but few chosen* (Matthew 20:16 NKJV).

4. Inquire with the Lord before you enter into a battle. Pray. In a time of war, David's wives were captured and held captive. Before charging in to retrieve them, David inquired with the Lord.

"Shall I pursue this troop? Shall I overtake them?" he asked the Lord.

"Pursue, for you shall surely overtake them and without fail recover *all*," He answered back (1 Samuel 30:8 NKJV).

In my bible, the word *all* is italicized, meaning there is emphasis on all! If we seek Him first, God will keep no good thing from us (Psalm 84:11).

There are only four steps here because four is a number commonly associated with creation. There are four corners of the Earth, four directions, four elements, and four seasons. When you follow these four steps, you're preparing to create, innovate, and walk into your miracle. You will walk in your authority, claim your victory, and expect to receive what is rightfully yours. No matter what it looks like, know God has your back. He will finish what He started.

**Reference**

And he said, "Listen, all you of Judah and you inhabitants of Jerusalem, and you, King Jehoshaphat! Thus says the Lord to you: 'Do not be afraid nor dismayed because of this great multitude, for the battle is not yours, but God's . . .'"

– 2 Chronicles 20:15 (NKJV)

## Day 48: I Come In Peace

**Listen**

Sia – Elastic Heart (2014)

**Read**

Be vigilant of those who claim to come in peace. Ironically, people fight for peace. The reason being, peace is a valuable currency. For instance, many literary interpretations exist surrounding the story of Helen. Perhaps the most popular interpretation involves Helen's abductor, Paris, who was welcomed into the home of Helen's husband as a royal guest. However, Paris was disguised with a façade of peace. When her husband departed, Paris carried Helen off to Troy. Some story variations suggest that a few Greek soldiers didn't wish to go to war to retrieve Helen. Just imagine if their wish came true. This inaction would be a sign of weakness. Other nations would undoubtedly notice the flashing red target on Sparta.

*Single Ladies*, be mindful of the people who enter your life. The enemy sends deceitful men, dishonest women, and even fraudulent prophets falsely promising you peace and blessings (Jeremiah 8:10-12; Jeremiah 23:16-18).

Jesus warned, *for false christs and false prophets will rise and show great signs and wonders to deceive, if possible, even the elect* (Matthew 24:24 NKJV).

Many will come claiming the end of times in Jesus' name

(Matthew 24:5-6). Don't become distraught, only God knows the time when this Earth shall pass away (Matthew 25:13).

You may have heard your grandmother or even your great-grandmother speak on the end of times. She wanted you to realize the importance of always being prepared, so you are not misled. You may think many generations of people spoke on the end of times and it still has not come. You have time, right? Not exactly, as each day passes we are one day closer to the end of times. Then even if the end of the times doesn't come in our lifetime, we understand tomorrow is not promised. We should operate like the five wise virgins, who prepared to meet their groom, bringing oil to light their lamps (Matthew 25:4). The five foolish virgins did not bring oil (Matthew 25:2-3). When it came time to meet the groom, they had to search for oil to light their lamps (Matthew 25:2-3). When they returned from searching, they couldn't gain access through the wedding doors (Matthew 25:9-12). Don't leave your oil at home, *Single Ladies*, and don't allow the enemy to break you.

What happens to a rubber band once it breaks? It's useless, right? You throw it away. The enemy desires to break your rubber band. He wants to stretch your rubber band to its full elastic potential. He thinks breaking your rubber band will seal your fate in a garbage can. That means like the foolish virgins you won't have access to the Kingdom of Heaven (Matthew 25:11-12). If you want to avoid this possibility, find your peace in the only true source for peace. Find your unadulterated peace in God.

**Reference**

Depart from evil and do good;

Seek peace [in God] and pursue it.

– Psalm 34:14 (NKJV)

# Day 49: Stranger Danger

**Listen**

Goyte – Somebody That I Used To Know (2011)

**Read**

Consider the story of a young lady; she met an American guy in a European college study abroad program. She hit it off with him great and they agreed to travel Europe together. They traveled all over the continent making stops in Spain, Italy, France, the United Kingdom, Ireland, and Germany. When each returned home, they lived in neighboring states, less than an hour apart. While home, she spoke with him once, maybe twice, but she never saw him again. He slowly faded into the background noise of her regularly scheduled programming.

Remember the last time, you found yourself crushing on someone. Then you discovered the interest is mutual. You befriend each other, and you talk every day. You go out to parks and outdoor eateries on sunshiny days, you hangout in the house, watching movies together on rainy days. These days continue and turn to months or maybe even years. Then one day you just slowly begin to distance yourself, you conveniently miss his calls and never call back. You never go back to the days of old. Eventually, you don't speak at all. He becomes a stranger to you.

Maybe your story isn't so amicable, instead of a peaceful,

natural separation, one day an argument ensues, followed by another, and then another. You realize nothing is being resolved. You decide to go your separate ways, but remain friends. Until one day, you try to reach out to your friend. You call and text him for a few days, but he never responds. You decide to pay him a visit at his house. You think, maybe something terrible has happened, and he needs your help. You arrive there, his car is in the driveway, the blinds are open, and the lights are on. You know he is home, but he pretends that he's not. You knock, and then bang on the door, pleading with him to let you in, but he never answers the door, so you mournfully depart.

Can you imagine if God treated us this way? Well, Jesus warned us in the book of Matthew, that some may experience this tragic destiny. Only unlike your friend, God will answer the door. He will tell you to depart, and state, "I never knew you" (Matthew 7:23 NKJV).

Do you want to be one of these people? I certainly don't. To avoid this fate, desire to live in His will genuinely.

**Reference**

"Many will say to Me in that day, 'Lord, Lord, have we not prophesied in Your name, cast out demons in Your name, and done many wonders in Your name?' And then I will declare to them, 'I never knew you; depart from Me, you who practice lawlessness!'"
– Matthew 7:22-23 (NKJV)

# Day 50: The Tightrope

**Listen**

Coldplay – Paradise (2011)

**Read**

You can go scouring the Earth for paradise, but you won't find it here. You won't find it in home ownership, an awesome career, a high-class salary, a husband, or children. Paradise is in Heaven. How do we know if Paradise is even real? As we believe in Jesus, we believe in His teachings. One of his last lessons before death transpired on the cross.

Before Jesus died on the cross for our sins, He spoke of Paradise (Luke 23:43). Some may forget that two criminals were crucified alongside Jesus. One of the criminals ridiculed Jesus, but the other protested on Jesus' behalf (Luke 23:39-42), and Jesus said to him, "Assuredly, I say to you, today you will be with Me in Paradise" (Luke 23:43 NKJV).

When I was in grade school, my friends and I loved making origami fortunetellers. Only a color and a number would seal our future fate. Would I be rich? Would I be successful? Would I own a home? Would I be married to the 5th grader in Mrs. Smith's class? Would I have 2 or 10 kids? Would I be a traveling artist, or an acrobat in the circus? Of course, we incorporated some misfortunes in the mix for entertainment purposes.

At such a young age, I was anxious for my future. Are you anxious for tomorrow, or worried about your future? Are you overly obsessed about your earthly needs like food, shelter, and clothes? Earthly concerns will not buy you a ticket into Heaven. Be confident that God will supply all your needs (Matthew 6:33). Did you know the gate to Paradise is narrow and not easily obtained (Matthew 7:14)? If you can imagine, the narrow path is like walking a tightrope. You must support your own weight to walk across, but the path is so narrow you don't have room to lift your arms for balance. In hindsight, if I listened to my fortuneteller and actually became an acrobat, I would have the skills to balance on the tightrope to Heaven. All joking aside, make up in your mind that you will not obsess over your worldly material needs; it may cause you to lose sight of the actual goal–the goal of Paradise.

## Reference

"He who has an ear, let him hear what the Spirit says to the churches. To him who overcomes I will give to eat from the tree of life, which is in the midst of the Paradise of God."

– Revelation 2:7 (NKJV)

## Day 51: One Out Of 7 Billion

**Listen**

Sara Bareilles – I Choose You (2013)

**Read**

Capture this moment to contemplate the concept of marriage. There are over 7 billion people in this world, but two people mutually decide to legally bind themselves to each other for the rest of their lives. These people are choosing one person out of 7 billion. Crazy, isn't it?

Let's evaluate this; there are so many decision paths you can choose in this world. You can choose extraordinary success, or conventional pleasures. You can choose to chase after riches, or simply long for wealth. You can choose to devout your life to your career, or to raise children. Yet and still, none of these decisions are as absolute as the decision of marriage. You can acquire success, but still enjoy life's simple pleasures. You can seek riches, but still dream of wealth. If you have an amazing career, you can still raise a family. Inversely, marriage requires that you denounce all other choices.

Replicate the concept of marriage to your relationship with God. With no hesitation, you should accept God into your life, denying any other gods (Exodus 20:3). Worldly desires like premarital sex and drugs can serve as gods in your life too. Make the choice to cast down all other options and choose God. God doesn't support divorce in a marriage, but He does support your divorce from the world. If you need to verbally voice to the world that your relationship is over, do it. If you have to put it in writing, do that. Inform the world you're separating from it. Then choose to remarry God with no hesitation.

**Reference**

You shall have no other gods before Me.

– Exodus 20:3 (NKJV)

# Day 52: To Be? Or Just Not Be?

**Listen**

Katy Perry – Teenage Dream (2010)

**Read**

Romeo and Juliet is one of the most popular teenage dreams turned tragic nightmare. Many adaptations of this tragedy have been fabricated, but none as well known as the original Shakespeare. These two star-crossed lovers didn't stand a chance against their own families or their own desires. Neither one of them lacked the capacity to logically solve their problems. However, can you blame them? They were only teenagers, young, and unfortunately dumb in *love*. Underneath all the beautiful words and ideals, Romeo and Juliet were superficial.

In my teenage years, my eyes sighted the most unappealing duckling in the pond–me. My high school was superficial and being that I wasn't popular no teenage boy would dare a second glance at me. Given these circumstances, I would long for any boy to express an interest in me. I reached a certain point in all my naivetés. That point was rock bottom. The day I promised myself I would accept the next boy who gave me the time of day. I would accept him as my first boyfriend, no matter his looks or creed. Of course, when a handful of teenage boys communicated interest, I broke my promise. I was desperate, but still had the nerve to be picky.

Eventually, I reached the age of legal adulthood and ever since, more than a few handfuls of men expressed an interest in me, but not one desired a commitment to love me. I didn't understand their apprehension. Until I realized all these men were living in a superficial teenage dream and they were not alone. I was living in my own irrational teenage dream. When I became completely honest with myself, I accepted the truth of the matter. My compatibility level with these men was extremely low. For one, none were true men of God; a quality I claimed was number one on my list. In reality, I was living in an illusion most of my early adult life. My thought process rationalized something was wrong with me or something was wrong with the men. Truth is these men had puzzle pieces that didn't fit in my puzzle. That was the reality.

If you can relate, *Single Ladies*, don't allow an illusion of reality to cloud your judgment. Don't live in a superficial teenage dream. Many illusionary circumstances may come in your direction, but don't dwell on these circumstances. Instead, remember to be watchful and pray (Luke 21:36).

## Reference

"Watch therefore, and pray always that you may be counted worthy to escape all these things that will come to pass, and to stand before the Son of Man."

– Luke 21:36 (NLT)

## Day 53: Once Upon A Time

**Listen**

Meghan Trainor – Dear Future Husband (2015)

**Read**

What's a fairy tale? Once upon a time, you meet a prince, you fall into distress, and he saves the day. Then you two fall in love and live happily ever after. This is the synopsis, but what's the reality? Love takes energy, patience, and time. It's not achieved over the course of 90 minutes like a Disney princess movie. *Single Ladies*, many of us have a fictional ideal of love. We think our husband should accept our every attitude and crazy thought without question. He should come bearing a house, a college education, and not merely a job, but a career. If you're like me, you prayed for a man, who is 6'2" tall with no kids. Obviously, God can grant these desires, but he's also not a genie. We're *Singles Ladies*, so we know we have favor, but God is not out roaming the Earth, granting us three wishes. The number one wish on your list may be a tall, dark, and handsome man, who falls head over heels in love with you, but even Aladdin's genie made Rule #2 painfully clear. The genie could not grant a wish to make anybody fall in love. Makes you wonder, are you being realistic?

As you know, I surround myself with women who are in a different position than myself. A wise married woman once shared with me if I desire a husband, *act it into existence*. You may hear people say, speak your blessing into existence, but perhaps you never heard act it into existence. If you desire a husband, sleep on one side of the bed. It doesn't matter, left or right, you choose, but sleep on that side of the bed every night. Do not plop yourself in the middle and spread both legs out. If your husband were in the bed with you, where would he sleep if you did that? Tell him good night. I'm serious tell your future husband good night. No one will think you're crazy if you're the only one in the bed anyway.

Have you ever prayed for your future husband? Not praying that he comes to you with his good looks or decent bearings, but really prayed for him. If not, pray for his well-being and his relationship with God. Pray that he makes the right decisions and those decisions line up with the will of God. I understand now these are the kind of prayers you should pray concerning a future husband. I was limiting God when I prayed for materialistic things concerning my future husband. Whoever he is, God knows him and He designed him for me. I don't need to pray for his wrapped packaging. If he comes with children, or no children, if he's college educated or not, he is still beautifully and wonderfully made by God and I will accept God's beautiful work. Will you?

**Reference**

I will praise You, for I am fearfully and wonderfully made;

Marvelous are Your works,

And that my soul knows very well.

– Psalm 139:14 (NKJV)

# Day 54: What's An Upgrade?

**Listen**

Beyoncé feat. Jay Z – Upgrade U [Clean] (2007)

**Read**

As *Single Ladies,* we like to think that we can upgrade any man. We can complement him just as well if not better than an Audemars Piguet watch. Honestly, what even defines an upgrade? Once I traveled on a business trip with three other colleagues. The trip was planned weeks in advance. The flights were booked and the rental SUV was reserved. We were all prepared to take care of business, and maybe even enjoy ourselves a bit after working hours, at least we thought. On the first day of arrival, we reached the rental car facility's entrance. As the rental car shuttle drove onto the lot, we noticed all the available SUV's lined up along the gate. When we reached the rental counter, the attendant had a different story. All the SUV's were sold out, but good news, the facility had an upgrade for us! We were offered an upgrade from a SUV to a minivan! We looked at each other and all agreed this didn't sound like an upgrade. We had several failed attempts to request that the facility honor our reservation, and then my colleague grew frustrated.

She passionately, yet decisively exclaimed, "What's an upgrade? It's just a word!"

I laughed, until I was able to compose myself in agreement. She was right; *upgrade* is just a word. Everyone interprets words differently. A minivan is not my idea of an upgrade, but the rental car attendant certainly thought it sounded appealing. My idea of an upgrade is not necessarily your idea of an upgrade. It's just a word. What are words? What is sickness? It's a word. What is heartbreak? It's a word. What's depression? It's a word. From God's vantage point, you have authority over all these words. You have **victory** over all these words. You have to claim your victory and walk in your breakthrough understanding God always finishes His work (Philippians 1:6).

God calls us to upgrade each other—that is man, woman, or child. God called us to upgrade each other for the purpose of sharing the news of Christ (Philippians 1:3-5). Once I had the biggest crush on a friend of a friend. Of course, he just had to have a girlfriend. My friend revealed that I was not the only one crushing. He was crushing on me too. Since we only shared our one mutual friend, I would only see him every so often. I attended my friend's birthday party and he undoubtedly was in attendance. Only this time, he brought along a plus one—his girlfriend. After being in her presence for a few hours, the verdict was in. In my mind, I ruled her a complete scatterbrain. At my first opportunity, I secretly, yet confidently, informed him, "I can upgrade you."

In hindsight, I should have reserved my verdict. As women, we shouldn't compare ourselves to each other. Instead, God called us to hold each other accountable.

We need to upgrade each other and pray for each other (Philippians 1:4). Even if our own definition of *upgrade* differs, we must remember God's definition of upgrade and follow it.

## Reference

Whenever I pray, I make my requests for all of you with joy, for you have been my partners in spreading the Good News about Christ from the time you first heard it until now. And I am certain that God, who began the good work within you, will continue his work until it is finally finished on the day when Christ Jesus returns.

– Philippians 1:4-6 (NLT)

# Day 55: Marvel

**Listen**

Trey Songz – Wonder Woman (2007)

**Read**

I never aspired to be Wonder Woman. It wasn't appealing to me for a man to *wonder* about me. I aspired to possess all the qualities that are clear and concise. Some men may view Wonder Woman as mysterious, yet enticing or day dreamy, but a wonder woman doesn't allow a man to gain close enough proximity to her to learn the real her. If personal space is eighteen inches to four feet, wonder women keep men far at bay. She keeps them away at least 10 feet or more, so men can *marvel* at her beauty when she's not even a Marvel superhero. Men just sit back in awe and wonder what it's like to know her.

I have to wonder, what even makes Wonder Woman famous? You have Superwoman; of course, her name speaks for her reputation. You have Batgirl; she fought crime alongside Batman and Robin. However, who is Wonder Woman exactly? I'm by no means a comic enthusiast, but if a man ever asked, if I were his wonder woman without a doubt my response would be a resounding no! Here's why, a God-fearing woman should not aspire to be a wonder woman. Instead, aspire to be a virtuous woman, a woman who is definite, consistent, and leaning on the promises of God. You don't have to swear by anything, Jesus told us the importance of being confident in our yes or no (Matthew 5:37). As virtuous women, we should learn that every *no* doesn't require an explanation. If you're uncomfortable, or you know you can't commit, exercise your right to say no. Non-clarity leads to confusion. Recognize who is the source of confusion. It's not God, therefore be concise, and be truthful. Essentially, don't be a wonder woman.

**Reference**

But let your 'Yes' be 'Yes,' and your 'No,' 'No.' For whatever is more than these is from the evil one.

– Matthew 5:37 (NKJV)

## Day 56: Think Green

**Listen**

Alicia Keys – Superwoman (2007)

**Read**

Since the panic of global warming, sustainability has served as a buzzword that focuses on reducing pollution emissions, recycling waste, and producing clean energy. This is admirable. God has given us this beautiful, green Earth; we should have a strategy to protect it. Saving the environment is all fine and dandy, but who is going to save you? The world was looking for a superwoman, and without hesitation, you accepted the job. You do it all! You have a job, or go to school. You volunteer, dabble in a few meaningful hobbies, and you may even take care of your children– in some cases with little to no help.

If you're superwoman, you may question who is going to save you? You need to pay your rent, or put food on the table for you or your children, but you don't see anyone to call on for help. Who will make sure you receive rest after a long day's work of saving the world? You want to wake up refreshed too. You desire a newfound sense of clean energy. No one is available to sustain you. That's where you are wrong. Do you know where your help comes? It comes from God (Psalm 121:2). You may become weary and tired. You may feel overwhelmed, but your life is like a strong tree rooted in God. Your God always and forever will be your sustainer.

## Reference

Cast your burden on the Lord,

And He shall sustain you;

He shall never permit the righteous to be moved.

– Psalm 55:22 (NKJV)

# Day 57: Living In a World of Octobers

## Listen

Adele – Chasing Pavements (2008)

## Read

The morning dew is crisp. The wind is cool, yet brisk. The leaves on the trees are turning from green to red, orange, and gold. It's time for hot apple cider and pumpkin patches. It's autumn, one of my favorite times of the year. To celebrate fall's arrival, you decide to bask in its amazing glory. You're feeling adventurous, so you decide to venture to a corn maze. Imagine every wrong turn you make in the maze is a dead end. Every time you think you reached the end of the maze, you find yourself in another passageway, another spiral, or another dead end. You are forced to back track. You're tempted to give up on solving this maze. Maybe if you just sit down somewhere, someone will hopefully and eventually find you.

Constant dead ends in a maze are like chasing pavements, which lead to swollen feet, blisters, and an aching body resulting in weary and fatigue. Chasing pavements sounds agonizingly painful. What's the alternative to chasing pavements? Giving up? You weigh out the alternatives. You ask yourself if this is even worth it. It may not be so bad spending the rest of your life in a maze. Don't give up. Instead, seek another alternative. Chasing pavements or giving up are not your only options. You don't have to keep chasing after the same man or type of man, but you also shouldn't give up men altogether. Instead, change your prospective.

Learn how to detect good fruit. What do I mean? What fruit? I'll give you a hint. It's not apples, oranges, or pears. While autumn is also a time to reap your harvest, we're not discussing a fruit basket here. Remember we discussed how to recognize a man's intentions. His fruit will reveal his intentions. This man will yield good fruit. He will yield all nine attributes of the fruit of the Spirit: *love, joy, peace, patience, kindness, goodness, faithfulness, gentleness, and self-control. There is no law against these things* (Galatians 5:22-23 NLT). If he's not yielding these good fruits, he's a direct reflection of his seed. He didn't water or feed his seed with the proper nutrients to produce good fruit. Jesus enlightened us when He explained that a good tree couldn't produce bad fruit (Matthew 7:18). If the man is a good tree, his fruit will be good as well. Therefore, pay attention to a man's yielding fruit!

## Reference

You will know them by their fruits. Do men gather grapes from thornbushes or figs from thistles? Even so, every good tree bears good fruit, but a bad tree bears bad fruit. A good tree can't bear bad fruit, nor can a bad tree bear good fruit. Every tree that does not bear good fruit is cut down and thrown into the fire. Therefore by their fruits you will know them.

– Matthew 7:16-20 (NKJV)

# Day 58: Cut, Print, That's a Wrap!

**Listen**

Beyoncé – Best Thing I Never Had (2011)

**Read**

Our God is omniscient. He sees all and knows all. Daily, God protects us from the known and unknown. This is the reason God told us to trust in Him with our whole heart (Proverbs 3:5). Think of it this way, the director of a film knows it all. He understands the creative vision. Since he possesses this understanding, he is the one most qualified to select the cast and crew. He interprets the script for the cast. He manages the actors while also upholding the scene. He communicates the vision with the crew. He instructs them on the proper lighting, set décor, camera angles, and sound. A director *cuts* the scene; he *prints* it for the editor's review, and finally *wraps up* the finished product. As with a film, God will be our director if we trust Him to lead us to an award-winning motion picture. He is on the scene and behind the scene working His magic, sort of speaks. God is the director of our souls!

Have you ever heard pondered on God's *mysterious* ways? Imagine you wake up late one morning, your phone battery drained in the middle of the night, thus missing your phone's alarm. Your natural body clock wakes you up an hour later than your alarm. You jump out of the bed and rush to the shower; you move as fast as possible because you know traffic will be horrendous. To your dismay, you are still running exceedingly behind. You run out the door, jump in your car, and attempt to merge on the highway, and then you learn the highway is closed. The highway has a 14-vehicle pileup accident and the uninvolved vehicles can't pass because an overturned semi-truck is blocking the road. You must find an alternate route to work. At that moment, you realize if you were following your normal schedule, you would be on that highway right now. You reserve that moment to thank God.

You will not recognize all the harm intended for your life, but recognize God will keep you from harm (Psalm 121:7). Don't worry about the *lost* job opportunity, relationship, or engagement. If it belongs to you, no man can interfere with it. Be confident "the Lord will withhold no good thing [from you]" (Psalm 84:11 NLT). You will find perfect peace, when you trust Him fully and your eyes are set on Him (Isaiah 26:3). Do not focus on things that are not seen, but focus on the things that are attributed to His greater purpose; this is called faith (Hebrews 11:1). He will give you favor. He knows what's best for you. Therefore, embrace His perfect peace.

**Reference**

You will keep in perfect peace
all who trust in you,
all whose thoughts are fixed on you!
– Isaiah 26:3 (NLT)

## Day 59: Holy Intoxication

**Listen**

Beyoncé feat. Jay Z – Drunk in Love [Clean] (2013)

**Read**

Being drunk can be a truly liberating feeling. You have cares, but you care less; or you have cares and now you care more. I was the latter. *Single Ladies*, I will keep no secrets from you. When I was sober, I could deny, deny, deny that I was over that man; I didn't need him and wouldn't take him back even if he begged. When I was intoxicated, I was the poster child of *Drunk in Love*. It didn't matter the hour of the night. I would call or send a text message because I always had something to say; now I possessed the liquid courage to say it.

Naturally, when life gives you bitter lemons, you desire a *chaser* to quench the bitter taste. In most instances, I did not drink with the intention of calling that man later that night. I'll admit, there were times when this was my very intention. The reasoning: those who are distressed act destructively.

King Lemuel shared this wisdom; "Alcohol is for the dying, and wine for those in bitter distress. Let them drink to forget their poverty and remember their troubles no more" (Proverbs 31:6-7 NLT).

God promises us life and wealth; therefore we have no need

to abuse alcohol in an effort to escape our problems. We cast our cares upon God (1 Peter 5:7).

In the book of Acts, the believers were celebrating at a holy festival when a loud noise derived from Heaven (Acts 2:1-2). The Holy Spirit emanated and flowed inside the believers, who began speaking in many languages (Acts 2:4). The noise was so loud; Romans, Arabs, Egyptians, Asians, and many other immigrants and foreigners rushed to discover the source of the commotion (Acts 2:6). The crowd of immigrants and foreigners were bewildered; the believers were praising God in their native languages (Acts 2:11). The crowd concluded that the believers were drunk on a fresh bottle of wine (Acts 2:13). It's ironic that these unbelievers correlated being drunk in the Spirit to being drunk on alcohol. It further supports God's desire of *Holy Intoxication* for you. Instead of becoming drunk on alcohol with the intent of being *Drunk in Love*, try being drunk in the Spirit. It's a liberating experience without tomorrow's regretful drunk text message.

**Reference**

And do not be drunk with wine, in which is dissipation; but be filled with the Spirit.

– Ephesians 5:18 (NKJV)

## Day 60: Exalt the Exalted!

**Listen**

Tamar Braxton – She Did That (2013)

**Read**

Is there such thing as being too humble? If God has done a great thing in you, but you don't share it with anyone, then perhaps you are being too humble. If God is not obtaining the glory for that great thing, it's time to open up your mouth and share the good news. Share your testimony, worship Him on the mountain, and exalt God in all His holiness (Psalm 99:9).

Perhaps you don't have the problem of being too humble. Instead, you ooze confidence. As *Single Ladies*, we should bear confidence, but be careful not to be boastful. Consider the blessing that comes with humility. When you have humility, God will elevate you (James 4:10). In this tidbit of wisdom, you understand the One who positioned you. God instructs us to *get* wisdom and understanding (Proverbs 4:7). Understanding this concept positions you as a woman of wisdom. Esther was a woman who understood the importance of acquiring wisdom and understanding. God positioned her perfectly to radiate this wisdom. Esther will be further discussed in detail another day.

Today, I would like to talk about me. That's humility for you, but seriously, I would like to share this testimony with you. As I approached graduation with my master's degree, I contemplated ideas for decorating my graduation cap. I worked full-time during the day, and pursued a part-time graduate program in the evening. I was proud of myself. I earned three degrees all before my 25th birthday. I considered decorating my cap with the phrases *Triple Threat* or *3 Degree Shawty*. Please don't judge me for the latter. Remember, *Single Ladies*, you already learned the importance of not judging someone. You're accountable for that knowledge. *As iron sharpens iron, [we] sharpen each other* (Proverbs 27:17 NKJV). This means we keep each other accountable of learned truths.

Nevertheless, I ultimately decorated my cap with the phrase *She Did That* in silver letters, and further embellished my cap with faux pearls and rhinestones. The finished product was beautiful if I do say so myself. I decided *She Did That* would be my anthem leading up to my graduation. On graduation day, I posted photos wearing my decorated cap on my social media page. Then, I realized God is not receiving His glory in my moment of elevation. This achievement is not just about me.

Correspondingly, I posted a social media status that read: "*She Did That*, but she couldn't do *that* without Him!"

*Single Ladies,* make every effort to ensure God, who positions you, receives the glory in all you do. If you choose not to give God the glory, you may certainly be demoted. Therefore, exalt the One who elevates you!

**Reference**

For those who exalt themselves will be humbled, and those who humble themselves will be exalted.

– Luke 14:11 (NLT)

# Day 61: Cast Away

**Listen**

Taylor Swift – Shake It Off (2014)

**Read**

Shake the world away! Take all your strain and all your stress, and cast these cares upon the feet of the Lord (1 Peter 5:7). If God cares for the small rabbit that hops in the meadow or the snail that inches up the tree, surely He cares for you. You are God's most beautiful and precious creation. You are His virtuous woman of God. People may try to tell you otherwise, but don't accept this as truth. Shake away all your cares and give them to the Lord because He is concerned about you. Shake it off. Don't allow negativity to consume your thoughts. As women, that's easier said than done. We're thinkers and our thoughts are often initially tied to our emotions.

As women, we may also stress ourselves over our physical image. We may watch our weight on the scale attentively and stress over that last piece of chocolate cake we shouldn't have indulged in. Do you allow what you eat or drink to consume your thoughts? Do you know God doesn't want us to worry about what we will eat or drink (Matthew 6:31)? Perhaps you're thinking she's joking right? Of course, you should still have wisdom about what comes into your body. Your body is a temple; you should take good care of it.

However, don't forget to be mindful about the things coming out of your mouth (Matthew 15:11). Ask yourself, are your words coming from a good or bitter source? If you find that your source is the latter, ask God to change your way of thinking. Ask for guidance in making those words intentional, positive, and constructive. Cast those bitter habits at the feet of the Lord. You will start to feel a sense of freedom. Imagine yourself taking flight like a bird: carefree and volitant. You fly to a place where you don't worry about those things that you can't control. You fly to a place where you don't overthink. You are a free bird, living your beautiful life!

## Reference

Casting all your care upon Him, for He cares for you.

– 1 Peter 5:7 (NKJV)

## Day 62: EXTRA-Ordinary

**Listen**

Brandy – Human (2008)

**Read**

Have you ever received an **extra**-ordinary blessing? One that defies the laws of what should be. A blessing that just doesn't add up using basic arithmetic. When you compute the calculations the total expense should be more, but it's less. You receive abundance, but the world says you should be deficient. You understand it's a blessing that only God's favor could explain. This is exactly what happened when He blessed one young woman with a brand-new luxury vehicle.

She walked into the car dealership thinking she would be walking out that day with a pre-owned vehicle. God had plans far greater than her own; plans so great that the brand new vehicle cost less than the pre-owned vehicle! She was so excited that she could not contain it. She wanted to share her testimony with someone. At the time, she had an interest in a guy.

She thought to invite him as her first passenger. It seemed like the perfect excuse to see him, and then still share her testimony.

She sent him a text message invitation, not revealing any details of her newly purchased vehicle. Hoping he would appreciate the surprise of her **extra**-ordinary blessing, he responded unenthusiastically and completely ignored her invitation. *Wow, even if* *he can't oblige as my impromptu first passenger, he wasn't even excited for me,* she thought.

Driving her brand new car home, she found herself upset. She would willingly trade the brand new car and run her former car to the ground if it meant having a man who genuinely cared about all the things that concerned her. If only she could have a man who shares in her excitement. If only she could have a man who loves her. She wondered often times, *is there even a man who could love her as she desires?*

She found tears rolling down her face. She pondered on offering all her material possessions in exchange for the blessing of a husband. Then, she realized this guy wasn't the source of her troubled feelings. Her own insecurities were the issue.

The young woman in the story was not perfect. She was only human. There are times when we all fall short (Romans 3:23). Occasionally, we wrap ourselves up so much in our own thoughts, consequently diminishing focus on the present. We think and overthink. Thus, disregarding the beautiful blessings God provided us. It's acceptable to remain honest with God. You can tell God, *I am human, forgive me Lord. I am grateful Lord for your present blessings.*

Understand *Single Ladies*, that God is capable of far greater blessings than material possessions. Perhaps your **extra**-ordinary blessing is not a car. Perhaps it's a home or a job. Whatever it is, if you can trust God for **extra**-ordinary possessions, trust him for an **extra**-ordinary husband too! The blessing of a car is just one thing God entrusted in the young woman's care. He may have also entrusted a car, a home, or a job in your care. God expects appreciation and glory for these blessings and He rightfully deserves both. God observes our faithfulness in a few things, so He can enlarge our territory with more *things* (Matthew 25:21). One of those *things* is a husband. If He can trust us to be grateful for material blessings, He recognizes He can trust us to be grateful for an **extra**-ordinary husband too!

## Reference

"For everyone has sinned; we all fall short of God's glorious standard."

– Romans 3:23 (NLT)

# Day 63: Spoken Word

**Listen**

Sara Bareilles – Brave (2013)


**Read**

Some of us are afraid to open up our mouths and speak. We may pray to God inwardly, but we are afraid to speak up outwardly. God has equipped you with the words to speak, but you're withholding them. You're withholding one of your most powerful tools as *Single Ladies*. You're withholding your spoken word! When you withhold your words, you may withhold your own God-ordained blessings.

If you're like me, Disney princess movies educated you on the act of bravery at a young age. Ariel bravely stepped out of the ocean from the little mermaid into a woman with legs. Belle bravely offered her life up to the Beast in exchange for her father's life. Cinderella bravely disobeyed her evil stepmother and attended the ball. In the end, these women received the victory of a prince, their husband. In all these instances, these women acted in bravery, but they did not speak bravery. Speaking in bravery is just as important as acting in bravery.

Are you speaking bravely over your heart's desires? As *Single Ladies*, we should speak in bravery over our desires by humbly reaching God in prayer. Speak to God and request those things in faith as if they have already come into fruition (Romans 4:17). Speak life and positivity over all things concerning you!

**Reference**

Watch, stand fast in the faith, be brave, be strong.

– 1 Corinthians 16:13 (NKJV)

# Day 64: LOL

**Listen**

Maroon 5 feat. Gwen Stefani – My Heart Is Open (2015)

**Read**

When your heart is open, you're open to receiving real love. This process begins with your *yes* to God's love. When you say *yes* to God's will for your life, God's response to you is *yes* for your every heart's desire and *yes* to His promises (2 Corinthians 1:20). God desires the same consistency in return. *God doesn't want you to waver between yes or no* (2 Corinthians 1:18 NLT). *This is the way of the world, who says yes when they really mean no* (2 Corinthians 1:17 NLT). Don't say, yes Lord, I'll follow you today, but tomorrow your actions show otherwise.

Let's talk about a common form of inconsistency. Can you guess three simple letters that can arguably be described as overused? What three simple letters do I speak of, *Single Ladies*? *LOL.* You're smart *Single Ladies* so I don't have to tell you this is a text message or chat abbreviation that began as a description for *Laughing Out Loud*. Nevertheless, here am I raising my hand to say, I'm guilty. About 99.8% of the time, I'm not laughing out loud when using this abbreviation. I'll be the first to admit I use *LOL* when I'm not sure how someone will receive my text message or chat commentaries. However, God dealt with me about this habit.

As you may recall *Single Ladies*, God says, "Let your yes be yes and your no be no" (Matthew 5:37 NKJV).

Learn to be concise; say what you mean without hesitation and without guilt. This doesn't mean do not have wisdom, or a filter on your words, but learn to say what you mean and mean what you say. You will find that people will respect you for your honesty and uprightness.

**Reference**

For all of God's promises have been fulfilled in Christ with a resounding "Yes!" And through Christ, our "Amen" (which means "Yes") ascends to God for His glory.

– 2 Corinthians 1:20 (NLT)

## Day 65: The Beautiful

**Listen**

Kierra Sheard – Flaws (2014)

**Read**

Not too long ago, we were lying awake at night questioning who was going to love our flaws. Now, we are accepting of God's faultless love, but we still may question why God would love us with all our faults. His reason being, He doesn't see flaws. He sees beautiful! Beautiful in you!

As a child, I would begin, and nearly simultaneously quit just about every extracurricular activity. The result: I *flawfully* had zero talent. In college, I was seeking a creative approach to express myself while earning scholarship funding. Competitive scholarship pageants served as that creative mode of expression. As I prepared for the talent portion of competition, my foundation was shaky. Singing reluctantly became my crutch. I always knew I could hold a note, but I was no Whitney Houston. I could sing, but not *sang*. I'm sure you know the difference, *Single Ladies*. If not, understand Whitney Houston was an example of a woman who could *sang*.

Even if you feel no personal relation to this story, a time or two, your ears may have painfully endured that one person who sings out of tune without any conviction. It may not sound like Whitney Houston to you, but God hears a beautiful sound. When you sing a song of praise to our Lord, it is a beautiful *sweet* sound to His ears. Therefore, no hesitation should exist to praise the Lord. Whether it means opening up your mouth, clapping your hands, playing an instrument—even if it's just a tambourine, do whatever you feel in your heart and praise the Lord.

Why should we praise God? Actually, the question should be why shouldn't we praise God? Think about it, if you're working on a challenging work assignment, or school project and you accomplish your goals with more than flying colors, would you appreciate some praise from your supervisor or teacher? Of course you would. Then why not give God the credit for fulfilling His promises, cleansing you of your sins, and loving you will all your flaws unconditionally? Don't worry about how it sounds, how it looks, or even where it takes place. You can praise the Lord in church, in your car, at home, and with or without music. Your praise is beautiful! Don't ever miss an opportunity to unyieldingly open your mouth and praise Him.

**Reference**

Let everything that has breath praise the Lord.
Praise the Lord!
– Psalm 150:6 (NKJV)

## Day 66: I've Got a Testimony!

**Listen**

Mary J. Blige – My Life '06 (2006)

**Read**

By now *Single Ladies*, there's no secret: I LOVE music. Consequently, I couldn't resist the urge to listen to both renditions of Mary J. Blige's '*My Life.*' Yes, you may recall, Mary J. Blige recorded two versions of this song. One was in the early 90's and the other in the 2000's. In those 12 years, spanning the two versions, Mary J. Blige evidently experienced *life*. My perception is that she grew, matured, and she grasped her testimony.

*Single Ladies,* you also will inevitably endure trials and tribulations. Consider the story of Job, he endured many trials and tribulations, but yet continued to stand righteously in God's sight. He was plagued with sickness (Job 2:7). His property was destroyed (Job 1:15-16), and his children were killed (Job 1:19). Job didn't understand his plight throughout the process, but in the end, his paradigm stood as an example for many of us who endure similar trials and tribulations. His story gives us courage to stand in the midst of troubles.

If you're feeling adventurous, I encourage you to listen to the original version of Mary J. Blige's '*My Life*' followed by the version listed in today's *Listen* section. It gave me chills. At the end of the

2000's version, Mary J. Blige declared a breakthrough from every past thing that previously consumed her. Be encouraged to follow suit, *Single Ladies*. If you're like me, you're not the same woman you were years ago, or even when you began this 90-day journey. You can reflect back on the previous days or years and move forward to the brand new you. The beautiful you, you have become! Don't be afraid to share your testimony with others, *Single Ladies*. It may just empower the next woman!

**Reference**

"I have told you all this so that you may have peace in me. Here on Earth you will have many trials and sorrows. But take heart, because I have overcome the world."

– John 16:33 (NLT)

# Day 67: Glory to God!

**Listen**

Mary Mary feat. Kierra Sheard – God In Me (2008)

**Read**

Don't be afraid to enter your *prayer closet*, fall down on your knees, and give God the glory. He deserves the honor for the mighty things He has done. He has given you life, breath, and another day on this Earth to live in His purpose. We understand for those who seek the Kingdom of God all other things will be added (Matthew 6:33). We'll have everything we need because God will supply it all. You never have to be ashamed of the things you possess; a nice home, a good car, or clothes, but don't forget to praise the Lord for His many blessings. Don't forget to give Him the glory.

Have you ever felt awkward or uncomfortable when replying to a gracious compliment? I have. I was having a discussion with a friend about how I desired a nomination for a company award, but I didn't feel like I was doing anything more than what I was supposed to do to deserve it. She reminded me that I didn't have to commit my time to mentor students, or go to schools and speak about engineering or technical careers. This is true, but I still recognize God deserves the glory for all my success. I now adopted a habit when people compliment me. My response is "Glory to God!"

It feels totally comfortable because I know it is God who has provided me with all things. After all, He supplies all my needs (Philippians 4:19), and then some. Perhaps the next time you find it awkward to accept a gracious compliment, try the response "Glory to God!"

### Reference

"Glory to God in highest Heaven, and peace on Earth to those with whom God is pleased."

– Luke 2:14 (NLT)

## Day 68: After the Hurricane

**Listen**

Whitney Houston – I Look To You (2009)

**Read**

Storms rage and winds blow and all at once you're experiencing heartbreak, loss, sickness, and turmoil. Hurricane Katrina has struck you. The hurricane left the pieces of your life scattered everywhere. You call your best friend, but she can't help you. You seek your mother for counsel, but she can't help you. Finally, you look to the hills; you look to God (Psalm 121:1). Understand the Lord is *your* help (Psalm 121:2). Learn to call on God first.

In the midst of every hurricane's aftermath, I would call my mother. This time was no different I was in a frazzled disarray. I called my mother and ranted. She listened attentively.

"What should I do?" I ended my rant with the question.

"What did God say?" she asked.

I had to admit I did not ask God. I came running to anyone who would listen, but I didn't go running to God. Of course God can speak to you through other people, but He desires you seek Him directly with your questions and concerns. He wants the opportunity to answer you without the middleman. If I went to God first, I would have realized that I didn't even have to run to reach Him. He promises to lead me down the paths of righteousness. He will comfort me even when the sun is darkened and I find myself in the darkest valleys (Psalm 23:4). I would know that when my mountain shakes, He is preparing to elevate me to another dimension. When I seek God, He will keep my mountains constant and steady (Psalm 30:7).

When you seek God, He will bring you over every mountain, beyond the valleys, and through every storm. Trust the Shepherd to lead you to greener pastures where you'll find rest (Psalm 23:1-2). Recall that you are found sheep, *Single Ladies*. Since you hear and recognize the Shepherd's voice, even if you fall astray in the eye of the storm, His rod and staff will pull you safely back into His flock (Psalm 23:4).

Once the winds stop blowing and the rains stop falling, it's after the hurricane that the rainbow appears. After I watched a film rendition of Noah, I was left quite puzzled. The only obvious accurate depiction of the film was the rainbow ending. I resolved, even if the film fabricated every aspect of Noah's story; at least it did not fabricate the rainbow. Consider the significance of a rainbow, the rainbow is an agreement between God and mankind; a sign that a flood will not destroy the entire Earth and every living creature in it (Genesis 9:16). The rainbow eases your mind, keeping you at peace. After your hurricane, God will show you a rainbow, your confirmation that God has not forsaken you. After the hurricane, you will find peace with God. Just look up to the hills, there you will find Him (Psalm 121:1-2).

**Reference**

I will lift up my eyes to the hills—

From whence comes my help?

My help comes from the Lord,

Who made Heaven and Earth.

– Psalm 121:1-2 (NKJV)

# Commandment #4

# Purpose

Thou shall find purpose and live on purpose.

# Day 69: Dare to Dream

**Listen**

Owl City – Fireflies (2009)

**Read**

God is the ultimate innovator. He created everything from scratch! Hey, He even created scratch and each of us was created in God's image. That makes us innovators as well. God instills dreams, visions, and gifts inside of each of us. When we tap into Him, we tap into our strengths, and this paves the way for our vision to come into fruition.

Find yourself in God's presence and you will learn to think outside of the box's box. Do as Daniel; he had a dream, and then he proceeded to write it down (Daniel 7:1). It wasn't until he wrote down his dream that the Holy Bible speaks on its interpretation (Daniel 7:16). Hence, write down your dream, the interpretation becomes your vision plan. Don't forget to write down your vision plan as well. Be innovative. Follow the plan. Revise if necessary. Do what is just and right to fulfill the dreams that God instilled inside of you. It may seem unusual to others, but that's perfectly acceptable. Everyone does not always understand things that are new and unique.

**Reference**

Then the Lord answered me and said:

"Write the vision

And make it plain on tablets,

That he may run who reads it."

– Habakkuk 2:2 (NKJV)

## Day 70: Apply Within

**Listen**

Jennifer Hudson feat. R. Kelly – It's Your World (2014)

**Read**

There may be some slight exaggeration in this song. As women, we aren't meant to be servants or slaves to a man, but the Holy Bible teaches us that we are a man's help. In the Garden of Eden, God saw that it was not good for Adam to be lonely (Genesis 2:18). To remedy this, God created the greatest creation of all time! Maybe I'm a little bias, but you get my point. God created a woman–a wife for Adam (Genesis 2:22).

A wife, who is *a help* for her husband, is a *Proverbs 31 woman* (Genesis 2:18, Proverbs 31). She gets up early and prepares for her family (Proverbs 31:15). Even now, as single women, we can practice being a *Proverbs 31 woman*. We can do things that are pleasing in the Lord's sight; do the things that are of good rapport. Wake up early, spend time with the Lord, and prepare breakfast. Plan your day. Go to work with diligence and purpose as if you were working to support a family. Show the Lord that you are deserving of this responsibility– the responsibility of a wife.

Why do this? Think about it, when you're seeking a promotion at work you first provide evidence that you are already capable of completing the required job duties before you are even considered for the promotion. The same concept is applicable for being a wife. If you want to be a wife, show God that you have the skillset to perform the duties of a *Proverbs 31 woman*.

### Reference

She gets up before dawn to prepare breakfast for her household and plan the day's work . . .

– Proverbs 31:15 (NKJV)

## Day 71: Be Fly!

**Listen**

Elle Varner – So Fly (2012)

**Read**

As a woman, at one time or another, you had moments of self-doubt. If not, you're one of these women, who *claim* she never experienced such a thing. You may relate to a friend or another woman who has expressed self-doubt to you. If you're honest with yourself, you accept that naturally, we have all compared ourselves to another woman physically or materialistically. You've had moments where you focused on her talents, her gifts, her knowledge, and her resources. We have fed into our own insecurities at least once or twice. Wishing we could fit into another woman's size 2; while that petite woman may be wishing she had our hips. As women, we fall victim to the comparison game.

The key is not staying in that place. Instead, learn to love how God created you! Focus on the belongings you possess and the talents and gifts inside of you. God has a plan and purpose for what He placed inside of you—your own unique dreams and visions. Don't trip taking a peek at another woman's book to the left of you, while still trying to walk forward writing your own story.

Jesus spoke these words in the context of marriage. *Therefore what God has joined together, let not man separate* (Mark 10:9 NKJV).

Let's look at this illustration in the perspective of God joining you together with your own dreams, your own visions, and even your own relationship with Jesus Christ. No man, or woman in this case, can separate you from what God has for you! Therefore, don't allow your own thoughts to permit a separation. Do what God told you to do despite what things may look like. God has a greater purpose. All *you* have to do is–Be Fly!

**Reference**

For I know the thoughts that I think toward you, says the Lord, thoughts of peace and not of evil, to give you a future and a hope.

– Jeremiah 29:11 (NKJV)

## Day 72: Lights! Camera! Action!

**Listen**

Jessie J – Who You Are (2011)

**Read**

Have you ever achieved something extraordinary? Maybe you scored the winning goal, received the leading role in the school play, offered a full-ride, State-college track scholarship, or in my case, won a local pageant title. I learned my singing wasn't so bad; after all, I won my pageant title singing the Pussycat Dolls' rendition of Sway. My first pageant sash bore the title of my university. Overnight, the campus student body and the local pageant community knew my name. I had social media friend requests from many strangers. People waved and greeted me via my name. I felt like an overnight celebrity.

When I returned home that night, I posted a social media status. I attributed God the glory for the wonderful opportunity to serve with style, scholarship, and success. The following weekend, I traveled to my first pageant as a titleholder. I arrived early to help with the stage setup so I didn't wear my crown or sash. I walked right up to the pageant's incumbent titleholder and introduced myself. I stated my name, but not my newly obtained title. *This fellow titleholder certainly knows who I am*, I thought.

Later on that night, I entered into the incumbent titleholder's dressing room to affix my crown, situate my sash, and slide on my 5-

inch heels. The incumbent titleholder looked at me and voiced, "I'm not trying to be funny, but who are you?"

At first, I was shocked. Then, I realized, not everyone knows who I am. I allowed the *stars of stardom* to blind me.

God will elevate you to higher places, but don't allow the limelight to blind you. Never forget the One who sent you, the "I AM WHO I AM" (Exodus 3:14 NKJV). Don't lose sight of the fact that you are a child of God sent to do His work. Be humble. You are a reflection of God. Be *who you are* in God.

## Reference

And God said to Moses, "I AM WHO I AM." And He said, "Thus you shall say to the children of Israel, I AM has sent me to you."

– Exodus 3:14 (NKJV)

# Day 73: Baggage Claim?

## Listen

Kelly Clarkson – Breakaway (2004)

## Read

A tug-of-war resides inside you. Do you feel the tug? You yearn to do more. You no longer wish to merely exist; you desire to live! That tug, that desire, it's called your purpose. It's the talents and visions rumbling inside of you, bursting at the seams trying to escape. If only you could breakaway, you would find your purpose.

When I graduated from college, I felt a tug inside of me. I was comfortable in my hometown, but a yearning desire was pulling me in another direction. That direction was east. In the Holy Bible, the east wind has a reputation of a strong, convicting wind (Exodus 14:21, Jonah 4:8, Ezekiel 19:12). The character of the east wind is best described as a whirlwind. My first visit to my new city delivered confirmation. God was indisputably leading me east in a whirlwind. He was already far ahead of me establishing an amazing career, a church home, and an apartment.

God needed to break me away from my norm. I understand breaking away from your own norm is not easy. It requires strength, courage, and bravery. On my journey, I attempted to relocate east, dragging baggage, instead of luggage. What's the difference? Baggage weighs you down; it's nonessential, while luggage is an essential accessory. My baggage was toxic relationships. I attempted to drag those toxic relationships on the flight with me. In a sense, God gifted me with noise cancelling headphones, but I wouldn't accept them. What I didn't understand was that wearing my headphones was essential to walking in God's purpose. Without them, I could not hear God's voice because the background noise was so loud. During my travels, I heard the airport announcements, the flight attendant, the pilot, and even the airplane engine, but not God. I quickly learned that I needed to wear my headphones if I truly desired to break away.

How can you break away when you're preserving the unnecessary baggage, and neglecting to pack the essential luggage? You will assuredly become tired and weary, but if you seek God, He will give you rest (Matthew 11:28). If necessary, He will carry you, but everything and everyone can't travel to your God-destined destination. You don't need to claim that baggage. Leave it. God will supply all your needs. He will give you his luggage, which is easy to carry (Matthew 11:29). Step out and make a purposeful move in His direction. For every burden you bore, and every tear you cried, God will renew you (Matthew 11:28). You will dance and rejoice (Psalm 30:11). All you need to do is break away and *travel* with the east wind.

**Reference**

You have turned my mourning into joyful dancing.

You have taken away my clothes of mourning and clothed me with joy,

that I might sing praises to you and not be silent.

O Lord my God, I will give you thanks forever!

– Psalm 30:11-12 (NLT)

## Day 74: I Can't Breathe

**Listen**

Jordin Sparks feat. Chris Brown – No Air (2007)

**Read**

Without love it can feel like you have no air and lonely air just feels like a waste. It feels as if every other woman is walking down the wedding aisle, but you feel motionless. You're not walking down the aisle; you're walking the world. How are you expected to walk this world alone? Understand this, you're not alone. God walks alongside you. When He's not walking alongside you, He's giving you rest. *Single Ladies,* He's carrying you.

You may recall when God gifted Adam the Garden of Eden and he had dominion over all the creatures (Genesis 2:15, Genesis 2:19). This responsibility alone didn't fulfill Adam. Adam was alone (Genesis 2:18). In Adam's slumber, God removed Adam's rib and created a woman (Genesis 2:21-22). We are familiar with this story, but we need to rewind, before Eve, before the animals, before the Garden of Eden, and before the Heavens and the Earth. Oops! We reversed too far. We need to fast forward, just slightly. Here, perfect! After God created the Heavens and the Earth, God created Adam. He breathed air into Adam's nostrils, giving him life (Genesis 2:7).

Did you catch that? You're waiting patiently for a husband to make it to you. You're waiting patiently for the man designed for you, but you can breathe! Why? Like Adam, God breathed air into you far before blessing you with a spouse. God created us from the rib of a man; the ribs encase and protect the lungs that process air, but God didn't give you a man's lung. Your future husband is not your air source. Understand God breathes fresh air through your nostrils into your lungs daily. When you understand this concept, you are prepared for marriage. You understand God is your air source, not your future husband.

**Reference**

The Spirit of God has made me,

And the breath of the Almighty gives me life.

– Job 33:4 (NKJV)

# Day 75: The Cycle

**Listen**

Marsha Ambrosius – Run (2014)

**Read**

Tears may fall, or may even run uncontrollably from your eyes, but in the end, you will find joy. Do you know the tears you sow water your harvest? Consequently, you reap the harvest of joy (Psalm 126:5).

Inevitably, as you gain years, you will lose people in your life, not because they have departed this Earth, but because like a seasoned plant, you grow up. I experienced a season when I knew it was imperative to remove some friends from my life. You know the type of friends I'm speaking of, *Single Ladies*, the male friends who are not *actually* friends in the platonic sense of the word. The ones you call on when you get bored or lonely because you're infatuated with them and the feeling is mutual. If I aspired to reach the next level in my life, I understood that I had to cut ties with these men.

I may have lost *friends*, but I gained heaps of joy and peace. I also gained the Sun. Beforehand, I could never get enough Sun because men soaked up all my energy. What do I mean? Do you remember learning about the photosynthesis cycle in grade school? You learned that the plant uses energy from the sun to produce oxygen for you to breathe. When the men soaked up all my energy, I wasn't able to store enough energy from the Sun. The men also consumed my free time, so I had no time to stop and smell the roses; subsequently, I didn't receive enough oxygen either.

Blocking my energy source was slowly killing me. I realized how critically I needed the Sun to survive. Do you understand? God is the Sun! If you bask in the Lord, you'll convert the energy you need to grow and flourish. God is the green thumb. If you allow Him, He will nurture your beautiful garden with ideas, ambitions, and visions that overflow. You will bear purpose and wisdom. You'll find tranquility and true peace in the Sun.

**Reference**

Those who sow in tears

Shall reap in joy.

– Psalm 126:5 (NKJV)

# Day 76: I'm On Fire!

**Listen**

Katy Perry – Hot N Cold (2008)

**Read**

Have you ever been involved with a guy whose actions resembled someone clinically diagnosed with bipolar disorder? Perhaps he was diagnosed. Regardless, isn't it frustrating to deal with someone who oscillates like a pendulum? In other words, does this conversation look familiar?

**Today 7:00 PM**

Him: I miss you. I am ready to give you my all. I promise this time will be different.

You: Really?

**Today 7:01 PM**

Him: Never mind, I can't do this. I don't know why I told you that I missed you.

Maybe your conversation doesn't exactly transpire along these lines, but you may have experienced someone who becomes hot quickly and then rapidly cold. First, he makes a promise. He is committed to you and your relationship. Next, his actions are not lining up with his promise. You remind him of his promise. Yet, he has no recollection.

"What are you talking about?" he asks.

You realize he suffers from amnesia; you're in for a real treat with this guy. He is convinced that he made no such promise. He assures you, you desired him so desperately that you fabricated a story. That's the only way that promise came out of his mouth. You must have dreamed it. He never spoke such words. Every day is an emotional rollercoaster with this guy. One minute he's up, the next minute he's down. One minute, he's black, the next he's white. Sometimes, he even attempts to turn the color gray. It absolutely drives you insane.

Can you imagine how God feels when one minute you're metaphorically on fire for Him, and the next you're lukewarm or freezing cold? Metaphorically, you emulate fire, all four stages of fire.

First, you're *Ignited*. You hear from God. He grants you a vision and purpose. He ignites you. Second, you fuel the heat source; you have a yearning desire to learn more and more. You experience *Growth*. He nurtures you. Next, you're *Fully Developed*. In fact, you're blazing! You find yourself walking in His glory. You reach your highest temperature at this stage. You're a vessel for God. Then, suddenly, you burn out. You become distracted or overwhelmed. Instead of seeking God as your heat source to ignite you again, you *Decay*. All your hard work and invested time is extinguished. Your *flame* is extinguished completely. The first three steps are destroyed in just one stage. You find yourself stagnate. You're not stimulated, and you're not progressing either. This is one of the worse feelings in the world—having the desire to grow, but you're stunted. Ask yourself, how are you going to avoid *Decay*, the fourth stage of fire? Ask God to keep you ignited, growing, and fully developed.

### Reference

So then, because you are lukewarm, and neither cold nor hot, I will vomit you out of My mouth.

– Revelation 3:16 (NKJV)

# Day 77: You're Hired!

**Listen**

Paramore – Ain't It Fun (2013)

**Read**

You're hired! Best two words ever spoken to someone without a job. Remember your first job? Do you remember your excitement? When those two words were spoken, you felt a rush of adrenaline. You knew all too well looking for a job was a job. All those days of searching came to a halt at that precise moment. Why? Because you found a job, weren't you paying attention? You're being compensated in exchange for a service; this is your first tangible badge signifying adulthood.

You're not a child anymore, now you must grow up. The same concept exists in the Kingdom of God. God is hiring for positions. Before you hear those two words, God needs you to grow up and accept responsibility. You may exist at a point in your life, where you are a babe in Christ. You are feeding on milk (1 Corinthians 3:2). Why? Your digestive system can't yet process solid food. If you're a child of Christ, you're eating solid food, but you still require some nurturing. Even, if you're a grown woman in Christ, you still have some growing to achieve. The beauty of life is that our growth in God our Father is never complete.

You have job security in the Kingdom. You have

opportunities for advancements and promotions in the Kingdom of God. God will not fire you. That means no unemployment line for you. You don't have to worry about being laid off or furloughed; you don't participate in any recession while working for God. You can quit, but I wouldn't recommend it. If you quit, how would you afford retirement? There's no standard 30 years to retirement, but you contribute to your heavenly pension or 401K plans with God. Your diligent and faithful investment inherits you the Kingdom. If you successfully retire, you will no longer work for the Kingdom; you'll own a portion of it. It's a lifetime commitment on Earth worth every year spent. You must commit to this relationship for life. Sometimes you will look up and realize it's fun living for God and fulfilling His purpose. There are times you'll come crying to God begging Him to make the world go away.

If you are like me, you couldn't wait to grow up.

My mother would tell me, "Don't rush it. You have your whole life as an adult, only a few short years as a child."

Her mother told her the same and when she was all on her own, she wished she were back at home. I actually never experienced that feeling. Once I was on my own, I never missed home. I embraced the joys of adulthood. I enjoyed my freedom. However, I understood my mother's reasoning. Being an adult is overwhelming at times. The entire load is your responsibility to carry. You can only depend on yourself, at least that's what it looks like at first sight. As I grew in my relationship with God, I realized I am not alone in this world. I can depend on Him. God will provide all my needs. He can do the same for you. Realize His grace is sufficient and accept the responsibility in the Kingdom of God. I promise you, God will take exceptional care of you.

### Reference

When I was a child, I spoke as a child, I understood as a child, I thought as a child; but when I became a [woman], I put away childish things.

– 1 Corinthians 13:11 (NKJV)

## Day 78: Round of Elimination

**Listen**

Destiny's Child – Bills, Bills, Bills (1999)

**Read**

Paying bills may be one of your desired qualities in a future husband, but what bills are you paying? Recall God's view on judging others. Can you pay your own bills? Perhaps your finances are flourishing. You pay your bills, you even have personal savings, a 401K, and investments, but are you investing in the Kingdom of God?

God instructed, "Bring all the tithes into the storehouse, that there may be food in My house" (Malachi 3:10 NKJV).

Are you paying your tithes and offerings? I will leave these questions for your own personal reflection.

Today focuses more on the matter at hand. We're discussing men here, and in the spirit of the late 90's, we are specifically discussing a scrub. A scrub is a . . . I almost started singing TLC. Let's focus; seriously, a scrub is a man, who doesn't want to work. He wants his mother, or maybe even you to support him. By no means am I condoning a scrub, but as women, we shouldn't reject a man because he's not a baller and his finances are not 100% in order. He may be living at his parents' home, but why is he living with them? Is he saving to purchase his own home, or did his parents fall on hard times? Is his mother ill? Is he her caretaker?

Life is not a game show; don't be too quick to eliminate a man as a potential husband. In the past, perhaps you were quick to eliminate a man whose finances were lacking, but have you ever eliminated a man for not being saved?

Jesus delivered this message as it relates to marriage, "And if a believing woman has a husband who is not a believer and he is willing to continue living with her, she must not leave him" (1 Corinthians 7:13 NLT).

We'll apply this message as it relates to a potential husband for a single woman. Imagine you meet a great guy. He has a lucrative job, a home, a sense of humor, a charming personality, and integrity. He is even kind and courteous, but he isn't saved. What do you do? First, pray and ask God to lead you. If *God* responds telling you not to eliminate this unsaved man, don't eliminate him anyhow because you think you know best.

In the first book of Corinthians, Jesus continues, "Don't you wives realize that your husbands might be saved because of you?" (1 Corinthians 7:16 NLT).

Again, as we consider this man as a potential husband, this man could very well see the Light in you and become saved because of you (1 Corinthians 7:16).

I once heard a true story of a 40-year-old virgin woman. She never stopped believing God would send her a husband. She didn't falter, nor did she waver. If she ever doubted God for a husband, she certainly never disclosed signs of doubting with anyone around her. One day, a genuine man expressed interest in her; only he was not saved. She wondered if she should even consider this man as a future husband. God told her to invite him to church. She listened and invited him. He attended the following Sunday and from that day forward he never left the house of the Lord. He never left the woman's side either. Unbeknown to her at first sight, the unsaved man was the woman's God sent husband.

The concept of being the Light in darkness applies to friends, acquaintances, and even at your workplace. You're possibly pursing other job opportunities with no avail, but you never asked God's purpose for your current positioning. John the Baptist was sent into the world to share about the Light, the Light of Jesus (John 1:5-8). Have you ever thought you may be the only radiating Light in that place of darkness? In God's timing, He will open doors for you to move.

Now, backtracking to the story of the woman and the unsaved man. You *shall* have self-awareness. Understand the word, *shall* from an engineer's perspective. *Shall* and *shall not* are used to express a command that must happen. Therefore, you *shall not* use Jesus' words as your clutch. Make sure you know the difference between not eliminating a man for the purpose of God's agenda and your own agenda. Believe me, I have affirmed my own agenda numerous times. Thinking I'm the Light for a man, but in actuality he was deeming my Light. Recognize the influencer; is it you or the unsaved man?

Finally, I will never say what God won't do for you, *Single Ladies*. I will ask you, what's the keyword in 1 Corinthians 7:13? You may refer to the scripture again. The keyword is *wife*. Are you a wife yet? Don't marry a man, who is not saved thinking Jesus told you it was acceptable. You will likely find yourself hurt, with an unequally yoked man (2 Corinthians 6:14). Remember, in 1 Corinthians 7:13 Jesus' intent is a wife, who was unsaved before marriage, and then while married became saved. Yet, her husband remained unsaved. As an unmarried, saved woman, don't marry an unsaved man, unless God voices otherwise. Even then, confirm that voice is God, double check and triple check. Don't marry that man if he isn't saved before you jump the broom.

**Reference**

"And you, child, will be called the prophet of the Highest;
For you will go before the face of the Lord to prepare His ways . . .
To give light to those who sit in darkness and the shadow of death,
To guide our feet into the way of peace."
– Luke 1:76, Luke 1:79 (NKJV)

# Day 79: Bulletproof

## Listen

David Guetta feat. Sia – Titanium (2011)

## Read

The enemy attempts to shoot you with heartbreak, disappointment, depression, and insecurities. You may be grazed with the bullet now, but you are not shot down. Why? You have God at your disposal. You may ask if God protects me, why can the bullet even graze me?

Well, I'm so glad you asked. It's because you're not equipping yourself with the full armor of God. When you are equipped with the **FULL** armor of God the enemy can't graze you. When you're following God, the enemy will inevitably attempt to attack you. The enemy may even attempt to defame your character. Despite the enemy, you are still a mighty woman of God. Recall the act of being humble; remember you are not greater than the master–even Jesus Christ was attacked. His character was attacked. Yet he didn't retaliate. He remained calm. He didn't sin in anger. He was titanium. He didn't allow anything to consume His energy or move Him off track from God's goal. We can't all be as humbled as Jesus. We have all fallen short of the glory of God (Romans 3:23).

I recall my most dreaded pageant interview question: what are your talents other than the talent you prepared today? I lightheartedly thought the fact that I was up there on the stage means I'm talented.

Since I quit just about every childhood activity I ever started, I struggled with this question. I would often resort back to being focused and determined as my talents. Most people would describe these characteristics as skills. Leaving me inevitably contemplating how I fell short and wondering where my strengths lie? Consequently, I decided to take an assessment to identify my strengths.

My result revealed my number one strength as faith, spiritualty, and sense of purpose, but I wasn't tapping into that strength. The foundation was there, but I wasn't doing anything with it. I always had faith that I possessed a divine purpose. What was that purpose? I had no clue. I would attend church every Sunday, but I wasn't making an effort to live in my God-ordained purpose. I wasn't giving God any time during the week. My life was fast-tracked in other areas, but my number one strength—my spiritual life was idle. When I starting tapping into my strength, I recognized the "joy of the Lord is my strength" and everything else fell into place (Nehemiah 8:10 NKJV). In my mid-20's, my *true* talents began to come to my remembrance. I recalled my love for writing and began writing *The Single Ladies' Commandments*.

If you feel you're lacking purpose, pray and ask God to reveal your strengths. Try completing a strength assessment. In your strengths, you may very well find your talents. When you find your strength, it weakens the enemy's attempts and strengthens your defense. When you are confident in your own strengths, you will surely become bulletproof.

**Reference**

The Lord is my strength and my shield;

My heart trusted in Him, and I am helped;

Therefore my heart greatly rejoices,

And with my song I will praise Him.

The Lord is their strength,

And He is the saving refuge of His anointed.

– Psalm 28:7-8 (NKJV)

## Day 80: Give to Live, Live to Give

**Listen**

T.I. feat. Rihanna – Live Your Life [Clean] (2008)

**Read**

Many people become distracted with religion over faith.

Religion says, "Do not eat pork, or fast every Tuesday morning before noon."

Faith says, "It's not what goes into your mouth that defiles you; you are defiled by the words that come out of your mouth" (Matthew 15:11).

God has called us to have faith—faith in our God-given gifts and God-given talents. We should have faith to speak to the mountain, tell it to enter into the sea, and believe it will come to pass (Mark 11:23). Remember, *faith without works is dead* (James 2:14-18 NKJV).

This doesn't mean we don't need to use the tools, machines, and equipment God provided us. We must first speak with authority, and then do the work in faith. Have faith and believe great things will come into fruition.

Most importantly, you need to make sure you're using your God-given gifts and talents for God's glory. *These are the gifts Christ gave to the church: the apostles, the prophets, the evangelists, the pastors and teachers. Their responsibility is to equip God's people to do His work and build up the church, the body of Christ* (Ephesians 4:11-12 NLT).

If you're having trouble identifying your gifts, ask God to reveal them to you. Then, apply your ministry to fulfill God's purpose. Recall how God called Moses to speak to the rock, but instead he tapped it (Numbers 18:8-11). How are you using your gifts? Are you sitting on them? Or worse, are you like Moses, using your gifts how *you* best see fit? Perhaps you're using your gifts for your own selfish gain. Be mindful of how you use your gifts. God sees all and knows all. Choose to bear the good fruit of the Lord, exercising your gifts for His good.

## Reference

Then the way you live will always honor and please the Lord, and your lives will produce every kind of good fruit. All the while, you will grow as you learn to know God better and better.

– Colossians 1:10 (NLT)

## Day 81: Honor Your Father and Your Mother

**Listen**

OneRepublic – I Lived (2013)

**Read**

Live your beautiful life! Be empowered. Be influential.

Do you know everyone must take an account of his or her wrongs before God at the end of his or her life? When you stand before God on judgment day, will He tell you well done my good and faithful servant?

The Holy Bible states, *the words you say will either acquit you or condemn you* (Matthew 12:37 NLT). This doesn't mean you won't make mistakes or slip ups; no one is perfect.

In the physical, you may break a bone, pull a muscle, or earn some bumps and bruises along the journey of life. When I was younger, I loved to outdoor roller skate. My parents always told me to wear my elbow pads and kneepads, but I didn't listen.

Consequently, I have the scars to show my disobedience. However, I'm not ashamed to show my elbows and knees. Hey, they are mine! You shouldn't be ashamed of your scars, bumps, and bruises either because they are the characteristics that make you exquisitely different.

By now, in this journey, you should possess a great understanding of your *Single Ladies' Commandments*, but these commandments don't take the place of God's commandments. I encourage you to read the Ten Commandments (Exodus 20:1-17).

Even as a grown woman, you should honor God's first commandment with promise, "Honor your father and mother. Then you will live a long, full life in the land the Lord your God is giving you" (Exodus 20:12 NLT).

I also encourage you to live each day to the fullest, not swearing by it, but just living each day in Christ (Galatians 2:20). It's perfectly acceptable to plan and see God's beautiful green Earth. Even if you're afraid of flying in an airplane, see your backyard; go to the local park, or the beach. Thank Him for His blessings; be grateful for the opportunity to live and breathe another day.

## Reference

I have been crucified with Christ; it is no longer I who live, but Christ lives in me; and the life which I now live in the flesh I live by faith in the Son of God, who loved me and gave Himself for me.

– Galatians 2:20 (NKJV)

## Day 82: Guiding Light

**Listen**

Imagine Dragons – On Top Of The World (2012)

**Read**

Stand on top of the world as the Light of the world. Be the lamp guiding the world in the midst of darkness and don't forget the One who positioned you on top of the world. God placed you there as the Light in your company, or in your department. For that reason, do not conform to the world's methods. Instead, be set apart as the Light, just as Jesus was the Guiding Light of the world. Besides, the intention of becoming the Savior, one of the other reasons Jesus came into the world was to be the model example of how we should live our lives here on Earth. The Christ life is not always intuitive. Thank God He sent Jesus to provide us with visual examples, and the Holy Bible is full of the most tangible examples.

Some people may say that Jesus is dead. How is He an example? As Christians, we know that Jesus is not dead. He was resurrected from the grave on the third day (Acts 10:40). On the day He rose, people were looking for Jesus in the tomb, but he wasn't there (Luke 24:5-6). He was and still is alive! Therefore, Jesus is the ultimate example for us. Although He walked the Earth a couple thousand years ago, He is still tangible today. Not to mention, Jesus is relatable. Before He began His ministry on Earth, Jesus worked a 9 to 5 just like most of us. He was a carpenter until around the age of 30 (Matthew 13:55, Luke 3:23). The day He began His ministry, He never stopped. He was never hidden. *Single Ladies*, you have the opportunity to stand on top of the world and live that example life too.

**Reference**

"You are the light of the world. A city that is set on a hill can't be hidden. Nor do they light a lamp and put it under a basket, but on a lampstand, and it gives light to all who are in the house. Let your light so shine before men, that they may see your good works and glorify your Father in Heaven."

– Matthew 5:14-16 (NKJV)

## Day 83: The Energizer Battery

**Listen**

Janelle Monáe – Electric Lady (2013)


**Read**

When God is the source of your life, you'll shock the world with your transformation. You'll walk into the room and command attention. Not for any doing of your own, but because the *Light* inside of you can't be contained. Your newfound wisdom radiates out of you. In fact, it permeates out of you. It seeps out of your pores and people are naturally drawn to you. You are wise, so you no longer self-sabotage. As a wise woman, you build your home up; you don't tear it down (Proverbs 14:1). Like the electricity in your home, you become the current that outflows all positive charges while negative charges move in the opposite direction of you. First and foremost, you place a surge protector on the electronics of your heart. You understand anything you allow to penetrate your heart will flow out into your life (Proverbs 4:23). Wisdom taught you to take the proper precautions. The heart's gateways are sensitive; you understand a voltage spike without protection can short your heart, causing you to go haywire.

People affectionately call you the *energizer battery; you keep going and going*. People surrounding you are static electricity, but you are the force that recharges and energizes them. You draw people in because you are impelling like a magnet. You attract people, who propel toward you with haste. You are like lightning; you strike with intention and purpose. People see you coming, and then they hear the thunder. You travel faster than sound. Your thunder is like the sound of a roaring lion, commanding yet compelling. Like the lion in its animal kingdom, you are majestic and you do not back down for anything or anyone (Proverbs 30:29-30). In the kingdom, others run away in fear, but *you are righteous [and] bold as a lion* (Proverbs 28:1 NKJV).

When Daniel was accused of disobeying a king's decree and worshipping God, he was sentenced to a night in the lion's den (Daniel 6:10, Daniel 6:16). The decree was established as a plot against Daniel (Daniel 6:11-12), but Daniel commanded the same attention as the one you possess now. The king was drawn to Daniel. In the morning, the king ran with haste to the lion's den to discover Daniel's state (Daniel 6:19). God sent angels to tame the lions and protect Daniel, not even a hair on his head was harmed (Daniel 6:22). Daniel's wicked accusers along with their families were not righteous people of God. They were condemned to the lion's den and the lions devoured all of them (Daniel 6:24).

As God tamed the lion in the lion's den and protected Daniel, remember the One who protects you. You have the eye of the tiger, but keep your eye set on the goal–God's goal. Your words should always remain purposeful and be spoken with dignity. God has graciously gifted you and you will be heard! Simply put, *Single Ladies,* you are *Electric Lady.*

**Reference**

She is clothed with strength and dignity,

and she laughs without fear of the future.

When she speaks, her words are wise,

and she gives instructions with kindness.

– Proverbs 31:25-26 (NLT)

# Day 84: Chosen

## Listen

Tasha Cobbs – Happy (2013)

## Read

As you approach the end of this journey, take a moment to reflect. Reflect on how good God has been to you. How He keeps you, how He covers you, and how He protects you from all things seen and unseen. He is an omniscient God. Recognize that He chose you (John 15:16). God knew who you would be before you were in your mother's womb; it was then He chose you to do His marvelous work (Jeremiah 1:5). Be thankful that He chose you.

You are God's chosen. You are His appointed. You are a precious jewel. Like the Israelites, *you have been set apart as holy to the Lord your God* (Deuteronomy 14:2 NLT). *Of all the people on Earth, the Lord your God has chosen you to be His own special treasure* (Deuteronomy 7:6 NLT). Recall God paid the highest price for you. Jesus gave His precious life to save you. That means you are valuable. You are a beautiful child of God. You should commit daily to bearing good fruit and living for God. You should commit daily to your relationship with God, and you'll find yourself falling deeper and deeper in love with God. Be joyful that He saved you. Be happy, *Single Ladies!*

**Reference**

"You did not choose Me, but I chose you and appointed you that you should go and bear fruit, and that your fruit should remain, that whatever you ask the Father in My name He may give you."

– John 15:16 (NKJV)

# Day 85: Smile

**Listen**

Tasha Cobbs – Smile (2013)

**Read**

Smile, *Single Ladies*! You already have the victory!  On this journey, we learned the definition of praise, so what's the difference between praise and worship? Why should we worship? Worship is surrendering your life to the Lord, giving everything you have over to Him, and denying yourself so you can reach His glory without any restrictions or roadblocks. When you worship you have a clear and direct path to God. You are no longer leaning on your own understanding. Instead, you're leaning on God for everything you need. A good worship song sets the stage for a sincere relationship with God. You understand you can do nothing without Him.

Worship also opens the lines of communication with God. God can communicate with you when you're open to receiving Him. Daily I learn to trust and have faith in God's revelations and insights, while not depending strictly on what I see with my own eyes. When God speaks His promises in my life, sometimes I am determined to convince God that it isn't for me. It doesn't fit into my life's *perfect picture*. Other times, I am determined to execute those promises on my own. Both are equally two extremes. I have learned that only through unyielding faith in God that everything He promised me will come into fruition.

In the same token, I have learned that I can't always share the blessings God has promised me with others. Often times it is not as extreme as Joseph, who shared his prophetic dream with his brothers who hated him for it. Many times, it's just simply that others don't understand God's promises for your life.

*"For My thoughts are not your thoughts, Nor are your ways My ways,"* says the LORD" (Isaiah 55:8 NKJV). You may not even fully understand God's thoughts for your life, and others may not understand it at all, but be faithful in waiting on the Lord who is leading you into His PERFECT WILL!

**Reference**

Trust in the Lord with all your heart,

And lean not on your own understanding;

 In all your ways acknowledge Him,

And He shall direct your paths.

– Proverbs 3:5-6 (NKJV)

# Day 86: Wonderland

**Listen**

The Walls Group – Perfect People (2014)

**Read**

Don't keep your testimony on the inside. Let it be expressed as light, not kept in darkness (Matthew 10:27). Sometimes that involves bravery. Many testimonies defy the laws of man, as some testimonies can only be described as miracles. It's not easy standing out, but remember, *[God] is a rewarder of those who diligently seek Him* (Hebrews 11:6 NKJV).

Be like Alice in Wonderland; don't fall in suit with the queen's deck of cards. What made Alice, Alice in Wonderland? Alice was not of Wonderland. She was a foreigner and it was obvious. She wasn't familiar with the customs or etiquette. She wasn't accustomed to being treated so rudely.

Remember, you're not meant to conform to this world. People will test you. People will attempt to convince you to follow suit as the queen attempted to convince Alice, but don't murmur or complain as the world. Instead, focus on strengthening yourself in patience and endurance. Be grateful. Just being alive is a true testament of a miracle! God loves you so shine, *Single Ladies*!

**Reference**

Do all things without complaining and disputing, that you may become blameless and harmless, children of God without fault in the midst of a crooked and perverse generation, among whom you shine as lights in the world.

– Philippians 2:14-15 (NKJV)

## Day 87: Trap Queen

**Listen**

Erica Campbell – I Luh God (2015)

**Read**

Christian trap music?! This was my first thought upon hearing this song. I thought this song was indeed derived from the modern-day trap music genre with its signature 808 drumbeats, southern originated sound, and jargon lyrics. Still in my thoughts, God rhetorically responded, *why not?*

Then even further thoughts ensued. I listened to trap songs rapping about my no flex zone, baking soda, and coco, when I had no personal affiliation to those songs or its connotation. I claim a personal affiliation with God, so why couldn't I listen to a trap song about God? Everything we have in this world and even the universe is because of God. He created the Earth and He created us. That being said, He can use whatever mechanisms He sees fit to reach His people. He can administer any creation of the world for His glory.

When God first revealed the vision of *The Single Ladies' Commandments* to me, I was on a flight, returning home from Las Vegas of all places. I tell you no lie. I was on a flight departing from Sin City. I wondered if the vision was God-given. I was definitely tired, but not hungover.

"Maybe I should get a second opinion," I questioned. "God

you want me to use secular music? Music of the world? The music the church elders warned against because it will flood our minds with lust, and corrupt our thoughts, that music?"

God responded, "Yes. I want you to dissect the music and extract the meaningful messages. Analyze and interpret the music the way I want them to perceive it, for its true intention. Enlighten my *Single Ladies,* so they perceive me in everything that they hear, listen, and do."

Then, songs and ideas began to flood my mind. I had no paper, or tablet on the plane. Even Moses had two tablets of stone to write down the Ten Commandments (Exodus 34:4). Documenting the beginnings of *The Single Ladies' Commandments* was essential. Thank God for my cell phone's notepad application. My notepad was quickly filled with the beginnings of the book's plan, purpose, and vision.

Understand this *Single Ladies,* whatever place God has positioned you, you are appointed and anointed to minister. You are a minister of God exactly where you are. He needs you in your very position. He needs you there to change the culture of your environment. You set the atmosphere. You're not a thermometer that merely reads the temperature. Don't allow anyone else to set the temperature, you are the thermostat, and you set the temperature.

In the book of Esther, God positioned Esther as Queen of many lands. She was the ultimate *Trap Queen.* In other words, she was loyal and resourceful. She was one *bad* woman. Speaking of bad, in a good way of course, Esther was positioned in a worldly role to perform the work of the Lord. God placed her strategically, and gave her favor with the king. Not only did the king favor her, Esther was clearly a favored woman of God. You may ask, isn't God impartial? He loves us all. This is true. He also bestows favor on all those who love Him and walk in His purpose (Romans 8:28). If you desire favor, like Esther, you must invest in your relationship with God.

Esther was favored as the second woman to have a book of the Holy Bible named after her. We learned the other woman was Ruth. God positioned Esther in the king's kingdom for the purpose of saving the Jews (Esther 4:13-14). The king listened to everything that Queen Esther requested and fulfilled it! Can you imagine a king accepting instructions from a queen? We have made great strides in womanhood to date, but imagine the views on women's roles thousands of years ago. In 2015, women were still tackling equal pay to their male counterparts. Esther's purpose attests that God can use you in any position. Like Esther, God has prepared you *for such a time as this* (Esther 4:14 NKJV), a time to live on purpose and a time to be the thermostat in your atmosphere. Don't miss your opportunity to speak up. Understand if you remain silent, God will favor another woman willing to fulfill His destiny.

**Reference**

"For if you remain completely silent at this time, relief and deliverance will arise for the Jews from another place, but you and your father's house will perish. Yet who knows whether you have come to the kingdom for such a time as this?"

– Esther 4:14 (NKJV)

# Day 88: Jehovah-Jireh

**Listen**

Michelle Williams – Believe In Me (2014)


**Read**

Like a *Phoenix,* you will rise out of every past situation, and learn to believe in yourself again. Imagine one of your happiest moments as a child, when you were young and innocent. A time before you were tainted with the cares of this world. Now think about the moment that all changed. God reminded me of the moment when Isaac was tainted. God tested Isaac's father, Abraham, and he obediently prepared to offer Isaac as a sacrifice unto God (Genesis 22:10). For Abraham's obedience, God provided a ram in the bush as an offering (Genesis 22:13).

God has truly provided for me over the years. *The Single Ladies' Commandments* is a true testament of Jehovah-Jireh, translated The-Lord-Will-Provide (Genesis 22:14). He collated my past experiences, stimulated my memory, and provided me with the words and the songs. I am acquainted with several people who embarked on the journey to author a book, invest years and struggle to complete it. Some just don't find the time. Some are distracted with the world's demands. While others experience writer's block, otherwise known as a gap in the story. The gap is the part that the writer has trouble filling. When God provided me with the vision to write this book, I recognized that God needed to share something important with His *Single Ladies*. There was no gap because Jesus interceded in the gap for me (Hebrews 7:25). Jesus is like gap insurance on an automobile loan. When you invest in God, but you still fall short, Jesus stands as a placeholder, *providing* you a direct channel to the Father.

I'll admit, in the beginning stages, I questioned the vision. I thought it might be too challenging to write a book; maybe I'll start a blog instead.

Those thoughts ceased when I realized God believed in me, He entrusted me with His vision. At that moment, I believed in myself and I became a willing vessel.

What's your story? Perhaps you dwell on the fact that you never completed your college education, or you think you lack the proper skillset, but the Lord will provide. Jesus will stand in the gap for you. When you walk in your purpose, you will begin to realize how God marries the gap with your every past experience. He was preparing you all along. Leading you up to the moment of epiphany, where you will live in God's full purpose for your life. Learn to believe in yourself because God believes in you. If no one else does, He does. Believe in yourself. Believe in God.

**Reference**

Then Abraham lifted his eyes and looked, and there behind *him was* a ram caught in a thicket by its horns. So Abraham went and took the ram, and offered it up for a burnt offering instead of his son. And

Abraham called the name of the place, The-Lord-Will-Provide; as it is said *to* this day, "In the Mount of the Lord it shall be provided."
– Genesis 22:13-14 (NKJV)

# Day 89: Right Turn

## Listen

Tasha Page-Lockhart – Different (2014)

## Read

Your friends do not recognize you. Your parents may not even recognize you. On the outside you look different! Why? You're radiating change from the inside out. God has implanted small seeds of *happiness*, *peace*, and *joy*. These seeds were watered and nourished; now these plants reside inside of you. Prior to this journey, you may have strayed from the Savior's example walk. You desired a refreshed and renewed relationship with Jesus, or you acquainted yourself with the Savior. Regardless of your path followed to this point, you made the *right,* right turn, now you're traveling in the *right* direction on the highway to *Different*.

      You realize now, certain men can't remain your passengers in your next season of life. A few of your friends can't ride along either. You're a new creature, so the people closest to you must *all* be new creatures as well (2 Corinthians 5:17). You've elevated, and fellowshipping with those who are like-minded is imperative. Being like-minded fulfills the *joy* God implanted inside of you (Philippians 2:2). You are no longer simply *Single Ladies*, you have transformed into a loving, healed, and free woman of Christ (2 Corinthians 5:17). You are purposeful! You must surround yourself with people who possess the same qualities. A Christian-based church is one of the best places to find people who have the same mindset as you, especially an age-based church group. These people can *empathize* with your daily struggles and challenges, and then encourage you. Notice the word empathize over the use of the word sympathize. We *are* called to sympathize with each other (1 Peter 3:8). However, an age-based church group doesn't simply have compassion for you without relating to your feelings; this is known as sympathy. Instead, these people understand your daily struggles because they themselves experience similar temptations.

Understand even Jesus was tempted, but He did not waver. After 40 days of fasting, the enemy perceived Jesus' hunger, and thus tempted Jesus to turn rocks into bread (Matthew 4:2-3). The enemy also encouraged Jesus to jump off a cliff in an effort to tempt God (Matthew 4:5-6); hoping Jesus would commit suicide, thus defeating our Savior. The enemy also offered Jesus control of the whole world; all He had to do was worship the enemy (Matthew 4:8-9). Do you see? Jesus can empathize with us too. Jesus Christ overcame all these temptations and more. Hence we are overcomers as well. We have the strength and ability to overcome just as Jesus did!

Jesus Christ may have seemed inaccessible to you before. You realize He's relatable now. Throughout this journey, you have developed a stronger relationship with Him. You view Jesus Christ differently (2 Corinthians 5:16). He is approachable because you have become a new creature in Christ. Fellowship with liked-minded people is essential for your continual growth even as this 90-day journey draws to a close. You will now embark on a new journey with your new mindset, and new people surrounding and supporting you.

### Reference

Therefore, if anyone is in Christ, he is a new creation; old things have passed away; behold, all things have become new.

– 2 Corinthians 5:17 (NKJV)

## Day 90: I Feel Blessed!

**Listen**

Jekalyn Carr – Greater Is Coming (2013)

**Read**

With healing and love comes your destiny. Your destiny is freedom, freedom on this Earth and freedom in Heaven! Your journey does not end here. The challenges you have endured and the hardships you have overcome in your life are no coincidence. The pain, the stress, and the bondage will be used for greater–greater thoughts than your own. Every page in this book is a true testament of how God turned every issue in my life around. Because you choose to accept His love for you, now *all* things in your life must function for your good (Romans 8:28). He did it for me and He's doing it for you! You have accepted salvation and God's gift of forgiveness. Every bad decision associated with your name has been erased; appreciate that your name is now associated with *life*, and appears written in the Lamb's Book of Life (Revelation 21:27). Take God's teachings from these preceding 90 days and your *Single Ladies' Commandments,* and apply them for God's greater purpose!

Consider this, the world says, "We love you because you are great!"

God says, "You are great because you love Me!"

He is great! His miracles are great and infinite! He is the very definition of greatness! Because you've walked into His greatness, you will do the same. You will have no choice, but to follow suit like a deck of cards. Receive your blessing of greatness. Go out and be a blessing.

We understand our ultimate reward is in Heaven. Nevertheless, recognize the signs and miracles all around you. Be the miracle He called you to be! Acknowledge the tangible evidence signifying your blessing here on Earth. The enemy thought you would never come out of your rut. He was wrong! No questioning here, you have truly been delivered! Your blessing on this Earth is your newfound **love, healing, freedom,** and **purpose**. Remember, this is only a portion of your reward. Live your blessed life, *Single Ladies*! I know I will certainly live mine. Your greater is here! You feel blessed and you look blessed because you are blessed! Be blessed, my delivered *Single Ladies*!

### Reference

"But you, be strong and do not let your hands be weak, for your work shall be rewarded!"

– 2 Chronicles 15:7 (NKJV)

You can find out more about

Jasmine Jones

and her books at www.jasminejones.co


Follow Jasmine Jones!

www.facebook.com/jasminejones.co

www.instagram.com/jasminejones.co

www.twitter.com/jasminejonesco


For information, questions, scheduling, or details about upcoming books in The Commandments Series, please contact the author at the email provided info@jasminejones.co, or visit www.jasminejones.co.

## About the Author

Author of *The Commandments Series*, Jasmine Jones engages an interest and love for contemporary music and biblical scripture in her first book, *The Single Ladies' Commandments: Songs for Love, Healing, Freedom, and Purpose* released in January 2017. In her short story, *"911" Emergency Crisis: The Day I Lost My Mind, Literally*, Jasmine vividly shares her transparent testimony of becoming an author and chief executive visionary of J Squared Productions, a business solutions company that cultivates an engineering approach to book publishing, marketing, and product development.

An engineer at a Fortune 500 automotive company in Detroit, Michigan, Jasmine earned dual Bachelor of Science degrees in Industrial Operations Engineering and Mechanical Engineering with summa cum laude and honors from Lawrence Technological University and a Master's in Engineering Management from the Pennsylvania State University.

Jasmine balances her many roles with time dedicated to traveling, writing, and STEMulating and mentoring young people in science, technology, engineering, and mathematics. As a result of her service to the community, Jasmine, a member of Alpha Kappa Alpha Sorority, Inc. and National of Society of Black Engineers, was the recipient of several organization awards. Formerly competing in Miss America Scholarship pageants, Jasmine was the recipient of the Miss Michigan Scholarship Pageant National Academic Scholarship Award and held the title of Miss Lawrence Tech in 2011.